Get Money for Your Classroom

Do you have a great teaching idea but no way to pay for it? No problem! A successful grant proposal can be the answer. *Get Money for Your Classroom* guides you through each step of the grant-writing process, answering common questions and providing examples from real, successful grant proposals. The first half of the book breaks down the "nuts and bolts" of a grant application; the second half introduces the author's MONEY TALKS acronym to illustrate ten important tips for writing a successful grant application:

M: Make Time
O: Obey the Application Rules
N: Never Start New
E: Everybody Involved
Y: Youth Input
T: Tell a Story
A: Ask for Action Items
L: Learn What's Funded
K: Keep Trying
S: Show Sustainability

Each chapter is full of examples—what to do and what to avoid—from the author's own grant applications. The book's appendix includes a list of national and regional grant programs appropriate for teachers. These helpful resources and the author's practical advice will give you the confidence and motivation to start applying on your own!

Barbara Gottschalk is an English language acquisition teacher for Warren Consolidated Schools, a public school district in the northern suburbs of Detroit, Michigan. In addition to writing many successful grant proposals at the local, state, and national level, she has served as a grant reviewer for the U.S. Department of Education.

Also Available from Routledge Eye On Education

(www.routledge.com/eyeoneducation)

STEM by Design:
Strategies and Activities for Grades 4–8
Anne Jolly

Two Teachers in the Room:
Strategies for Co-Teaching Success
Elizabeth Stein

Passionate Readers:
The Art of Reaching and Engaging Every Child
Pernille Ripp

Passionate Learners:
How to Engage and Empower Your Students
Pernille Ripp

The Passion-Driven Classroom, 2e:
A Framework for Teaching and Learning
Angela Maiers and Amy Sandvold

DIY Project Based Learning for ELA and History
Heather Wolpert-Gawron

DIY Project Based Learning for Math and Science
Heather Wolpert-Gawron

Math Problem Solving in Action:
Getting Students to Love Word Problems, Grades 3–5
Nicki Newton

Math Problem Solving in Action:
Getting Students to Love Word Problems, Grades K-2
Nicki Newton

Get Money for Your Classroom

Easy Grant Writing Ideas That Work

Barbara Gottschalk

Routledge
Taylor & Francis Group
NEW YORK AND LONDON

First published 2018
by Routledge
711 Third Avenue, New York, NY 10017

and by Routledge
2 Park Square, Milton Park, Abingdon, Oxon, OX14 4RN

Routledge is an imprint of the Taylor & Francis Group, an informa business

Library of Congress Cataloging-in-Publication Data
A catalog record for this book has been requested

ISBN: 978-1-138-10435-8 (hbk)
ISBN: 978-1-138-10436-5 (pbk)
ISBN: 978-1-315-10227-6 (ebk)

Typeset in Palatino
by Deanta Global Publishing Services, Chennai, India

Dedicated to
the students and staff of Susick Elementary

Contents

Contents

About the Author

Barbara Gottschalk is an English language acquisition teacher at Susick Elementary in Warren Consolidated Schools, a public school district in the northern suburbs of Detroit, Michigan. She has applied for many grants, implemented many successful grant proposals, and served as a grant reviewer for programs at both the state and national level. Implementing successful grant-funded projects is definitely the part of the grant-writing process she likes best. You'll find it's the part you like the best too!

Acknowledgments

I'd like to thank my sister, Kathleen Andrews, who read and commented on the first drafts of this book. My husband, Cemil Ulus, never quite understood why I happily spent so many hours at the computer writing, but always offered encouragement and support. My editor, Lauren Davis, believed in this book from the very first stages and provided valuable feedback. I'm also grateful to my former teaching colleague, Helene Popovich, who kept telling me to "write it all down" whenever I shared yet another teaching story with her. Finally, a heartfelt thanks to my former principal, Dr. Pat Cavanaugh, who started this process by suggesting, "You know, Barbara, you ought to write a book . . . "

1

Introduction

Why Write Grant Proposals?

I believe one of the best and easiest ways teachers can make an impact, both in their classrooms and beyond, is to know how to obtain funding for their own good ideas. I'm guessing you believe so too or you wouldn't be reading this! In this short book, I'll explain the basic parts of a typical grant proposal, give you annotated examples from successful applications, and share tips for grant-writing success, all gleaned from my many acceptances and rejections. A middle school principal I once had used to remind students that everyone makes mistakes. He'd go on, however, to point out that smart students learn from their mistakes, and *really* smart students learn from other people's mistakes. Just like this principal's students, you'll learn from the mistakes you make from writing even one grant proposal. Reading this book, however, will also help you learn from *my* mistakes. That's a faster and more efficient way to success.

Numerous research studies from experts such as Marzano (2004) and less well-known online authors Greene, Kisida, and Bowen (2014) have pointed out the value of project-based activities and real-world experiences for all students. One could argue these "extras" really shouldn't be considered extra at all, and that by looking to outside funding sources, classroom teachers are actually hurting their cause long term by enabling school boards and legislators to cut budgets guilt free. The reality, though, is school budgets are tighter than ever everywhere. Figure 1.1 shows average per-pupil spending for public elementary and secondary schools in the United States steadily increased from 2000 on, but has stayed relatively flat since 2008, according to the most recent U.S. Census statistics. Making matters worse, the percentage of students in need continues to increase. According to data from the National Center for Education Statistics, students eligible for free or reduced-price lunch increased by 14% from 2001 to 2013; 52% of K-12 public school students in the U.S. are now eligible for free or reduced-price lunch. Teachers themselves often try to fill the gaps. A 2013 Horace Mann survey of 1,700 public K-12 teachers found 58% reported spending $200 or more out of their own pocket for classroom projects and supplies; 81% reported abandoning at least one project because the cost wasn't covered by the school budget or by other sources. There's a better way—and another source. A successful grant application can fund activities that benefit not only your students, but the rest of your school's student body as well.

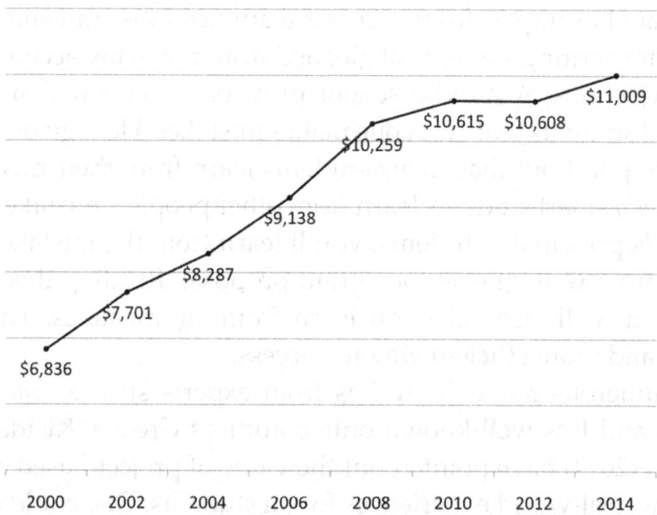

Figure 1.1 Average per pupil spending in U.S. public schools, K-12. Source: US Census.

Why write grant proposals? Well, the obvious answer is another question, why not? Teachers always need money for activities they want to implement in their classrooms and/or schools. It's especially easy for classroom teachers to write effective grant proposals because they know their situations well and can articulate exactly what they need. As a classroom teacher, you already have passion for your cause and knowledge of your students—this book will introduce you to the specifics you need to start generating good project ideas and writing successful grant proposals. And it's really grant proposals you'll be writing; it's a misnomer when people talk about writing grants. We *implement* grants; we actually *write* grant applications, or grant proposals. So many people refer to "grant writing," however, that I've surrendered linguistically and even used this slightly incorrect phrase in the title of this book. I'll use it in the rest of this book too. Just so you know.

I started out searching for grant opportunities as a teacher in my district's elementary magnet center for newcomers. Like teachers everywhere, I wanted to provide my 4th and 5th grade students with things like field trips and project materials that enriched and extended their classroom experiences. I knew these extras were especially beneficial for English language learners (ELLs), but nearly all my students were new to the United States and from refugee families with very limited incomes. It just wasn't possible to expect parents to pay much toward the cost of field trips and other activities. That's when I turned to grants for help. I was moderately successful at obtaining funding, mostly, I thought, because I could demonstrate a high financial need by my students. When my district disbanded its magnet program for newcomers and I became a school-based English as a second language teacher, I thought my grant writing days were over because I didn't teach my own self-contained class of students. In fact, however, my grant proposal writing was just getting started. Since English language learners comprised over 40% of my new school's student body, I found that working together with all the other teachers in my school on these students' behalf allowed me to think much larger than I had before. I wanted to encourage teachers to work together to try project-based activities that incorporated service learning and the arts. Being able to obtain funding for activities I knew would especially benefit English language learners allowed me to influence the curriculum and make an impact far beyond my own classroom. It's pretty hard to say no to an idea that has already been funded! Writing grant proposals also gave me opportunities to work closely with general education teachers to give them support through something concrete and tangible—money for projects *they* wanted to do as well. You'll find that obtaining grant money can extend your influence too.

"Are there grants for smaller class sizes?" one of my colleagues plaintively asked me once. Well, yes, there are, but typically they are large government-funded formula grants, so large, in fact, they are implemented by your district's central administration. These grants don't fall within the scope of this short book, mainly because I want to show you how to prepare applications for grant awards *you* control. These are smaller competitively-reviewed grant programs available to classroom teachers, typically with awards of less than $10,000 and for projects that can be implemented by individuals or small teams of teachers. Crowdfunding websites like www.donorschoose.org, www.gofundme.com, or www.adoptaclassroom.org are also available to teachers, but these are much more public initiatives dependent on social media for visibility. They're also more suitable for obtaining things such as classroom materials, school supplies, and the like. This handbook won't address crowdfunding sources specifically, but the tips you get here for writing longer, peer-reviewed grant applications can also be applied to writing effective blurbs for crowdfunding websites.

Preparing a grant application can bring you and your students financial rewards, but it can also benefit you as an educator in other ways. Writing grant proposals can help you see the big picture. As you prepare grant applications, you'll need to learn about the demographics of your students and your school—things like the free or reduced-price lunch rate, the percentage of English language learners, the test scores, etc. Of course, it's a big job to collect all of this information at first, but it's important to know for reasons that go beyond preparing the grant application.

Gathering this information will help you gain a better overall understanding of the larger environment in which you work. That's a plus for any teacher. It will also help you generate better grant proposals. That's a plus for you as a grant seeker.

Grant proposal writing can also motivate you, especially if you're goal oriented. You as a classroom teacher are best suited for grant writing for your students. You know your students best and what they need. Your interest, knowledge, and enthusiasm will shine through to ultimately create a better application than a full-time grant writer in central administration could. Getting the funds you need for the projects you want to implement is extremely motivating because it's tangible evidence of success. It's also concrete proof that somebody else also believes in you, your students, and your project; after all, they're supporting it monetarily!

Finally, grant proposal writing empowers you because it can extend your influence beyond your own classroom. We all know money talks; obtaining funds can help you implement your own good ideas without waiting for funding that depends on other people's approvals. In five years, I obtained over 50 grant awards for my school ranging from $50 to $12,000 through various grant programs available to classroom teachers *just like you*. Looking back, I can see that even some of the smallest grant awards made a big impact because they were sustainable and led to bigger things. What I can definitively say about all the grants I obtained, both large and small, is they helped me make a bigger difference than I could have otherwise. They allowed me to team with the teachers I supported to do things I knew would especially benefit the students I supported: English language learners. Even writing unsuccessful applications made me a better teacher. Working together with my colleagues helped me learn more about what they wanted for our students, and that, inevitably, led to better grant applications.

In the following pages, you'll learn about the basic parts of all grant applications and get tips for writing better proposals. Even better, you'll see actual excerpts from successful applications I have submitted to various grant programs. You'll soon notice I broke some of my own grant -writing rules in the examples

I show you, but that was precisely my point for including them in this book. I wanted to show you how good is *good enough*.

I'm not a full-time grant writer, I'm not an administrator, and I'm not in higher education, where the ability to get external grant funding is not just something nice to have, but essential for professional success. I'm a K-12 teacher just like you, and if I can do it, *you can too*. The information you get in this book will help you adapt your ideas and write them into proposals, whether you're preparing a four-page narrative or a simple 150-word request. Yes, we shouldn't have to write grants for things schools should already be providing, but if the money is being offered, go for it! Read on.

Quick Recap

You should write grant proposals because:

1. You need the funding.
2. You know your students' needs well.
3. It can benefit you as a teacher.
4. It can extend your influence.

References

Greene, J., Kisida, B., and Bowen, D. (2014, Winter). *The Educational Value of Field Trips*. Retrieved from www.educationnext.org

Horace Mann Educator Advisory Panel (2013, June). Survey. Retrieved from http://horacemann.com/teacher-lounge/educator-advisory-panel/~/media/Documents/Advisory%20panel/Expenses%20Budget%20Community%20Involvement%20Facebook%20Email.ashx

Leachman, M., Albares, N., Masterson, K., and Wallace, M. (2016, January 25). Most States Have Cut School Funding, and Some Continue Cutting. Center on Budget and Policy Priorities, Washington, DC. Retrieved from www.cbpp.org/research/state-budget-and-tax/most-states-have-cut-school-funding-and-some-continue-cutting

Marzano, Robert J. (2004). *Building Background Knowledge for Academic Achievement*. Association for Supervision and Curriculum Development, Alexandria, VA.

National Center for Education Statistics (2015). *Digest of Education Statistics*. Table 204.10. Retrieved from https://nces.ed.gov/programs/digest/d15/tables/dt15_204.10.asp?current=yes

U.S. Census (2016, June). *Public Education Finances: 2014*, xvi. Retrieved from https://census.gov/content/dam/Census/library/publications/2016/econ/g14-aspef.pdf

2

Parts of a Grant Application

Summary and Title

Many grant applications will ask for a project summary or an executive summary, especially if they require a longer narrative later as part of the application. Other applications ask for much shorter answers, so you may not necessarily need to write a project summary. Since nearly all such short-form answers are word limited, you'll still have to succinctly spell out the who, what, where, why, and how of your project proposal in as few words as possible. The dedicated project summary typically appears in the cover sheet or the first part of the application, not in the longer narrative. It's also relatively easy to identify this part of the application; it's usually not disguised as another, differently worded question. Here are some ways this question typically appears in applications:

- **Please describe your project idea in no more than five to ten sentences that tell us: Who, What, When, Where, Why, and How about your project. This is the most important question in the whole application—we will need to understand exactly what you are doing!**
- **Please provide a brief but thorough summary (ten sentences or fewer) of your proposed program.**

Think of the project summary as your "elevator speech" in which you pitch your idea in 30 seconds, or in the case of a grant application, in just a few sentences. Many applications will give you a word or sentence limit; usually it's just 100 words or ten sentences—in other words, a paragraph or two. Unless you're directed otherwise, it's a good idea to write the summary in the third person. That's because the funding organization may use your project summary later for press release purposes if the proposal is funded. It may also appear on the funder's website in future years to give potential applicants an idea of the kinds of projects that have received funding in the past. Another reason it's not a good idea to use "we" is because it may not be readily apparent to a reviewer who "we" really is. In fact, it's good practice to write the rest of your grant application in the third person as well. If you're preparing a large grant proposal, implementing a successful one will be much easier if it's done as a team effort anyway. It's important for your grant application to reflect this.

Here is an example of a project summary from a successful National Education Association Foundation Learning and Leadership grant application. This particular grant program supports professional development for teachers. The application required a 100-word project summary:

> The lower elementary teachers at Susick Elementary will work together to help Susick's youngest English language learners attain proficiency even more quickly than they do now. Kindergarten teacher Catherine Cushard will head the effort by attending a train the trainer institute at the Center for Applied Linguistics (CAL) in Washington, DC on "What's Different about Teaching Reading to English Language Learners." Back at Susick, she and Barbara Gottschalk, English language acquisition teacher, will lead a study group composed of their lower elementary colleagues, the teachers at Susick with the greatest numbers of English language learners in their classes.

Notice how this summary tells exactly what will happen during the project and who will do the activities. It also provides a rationale for the entire project idea (helping train teachers of young English language learners) and uses student demographics to demonstrate need by noting how lower elementary classes have the greatest number of English language learners. These proposal items were all included and explained in more detail later in the rest of the application, but it was great to get them in the summary as well.

Here's another 100-word summary for an arts in education residency project that was funded through my state's cultural organization, the Michigan Council for Arts and Cultural Affairs:

> Michigan Opera Theatre (MOT) will begin a project at Susick in January by performing *The Pied Piper of Hamelin* to build background for all students. A core group of students will then create an original opera guided by MOT artists in 15 sessions during the rest of the year. A classroom teacher, plus Susick's music, art, media, and ESL teachers, will participate, ensuring cross-curricular connections. A trip to see *The Very Last Green Thing* will help students polish their production before presenting it to Susick students and to residents of Cherrywood Nursing Home.

Again, this summary illustrates how it's important to be as specific as possible about the proposed project's activities, mainly because this indicates thoughtful planning. This particular program required the residency to be conducted with a core group of students, but the project summary noted an activity was planned for the entire student body as well. This is good since grant programs tend to look favorably on proposals that can benefit large numbers of students, all other variables being equal. This summary also mentions students will present the finished opera at a nearby nursing home, which shows the project's connections to the outside community. As specific as I thought this summary was, however, the grant reviewers noted the "core group of students" should have been specifically identified. I intentionally didn't identify the core group of students, mainly because we weren't optimistic about getting the funding. I didn't want to get a colleague's expectations raised only to have them dashed when the grant application was rejected. When funding came through just before the start of the project, however, quickly deciding on the core group of students was difficult. It taught me, and hopefully, it'll teach you, too, to be as *specific* as possible as *often* as possible as *early* as possible when planning your grant-funded project. If you do this, it will be relatively easy to write the short summary of the project. Some grant writers recommend writing the summary after the rest of the grant application is completed; doing so will enable you to easily include specific information. On the other hand, I often find it just as easy to write the summary first, especially if I already have a clear idea of what will be done with the grant award. That, in itself, is a good start toward a successful grant application.

Not all grant applications will ask for a project title, but if they do, its length will be limited. Use this opportunity to start educating your readers about your grant request by making sure the title is easy to remember and accurately reflects the scope of your project. If you want to buy materials, make it clear in the title and in the summary that what the students will do with the materials is more important than the materials themselves. For example, don't call your grant request "Flexible Seating" when over half the items your budget is requesting aren't seats. Similarly, the title "Flexible Seating" tells the funder what you want, but it doesn't indicate what you hope to accomplish with it. A better title might be "Flexible Seating=Student-Chosen Seating" or "Flexible Seating–The Power of Choice." In this example, adding just a few extra words tells the grant funders what will be accomplished if funds are granted for flexible seating. The project title for the opera residency described in the previous project summary was "Susick Students Learn to Sing a Story." This title wasn't particularly catchy or clever (which isn't necessary), but in just a few words, it captured the objective of the whole project—for students to create and perform an original opera. A good example of a more clever title is this one from a successful

Target Field Trip grant application for 2nd graders to visit a local aquarium: "Let's Go See Sea Life." It used word play, yet it clearly stated the objective of the field trip in language even 2nd graders could understand. Unlike the summary, the title really should be the last thing you write, mainly because I feel it's less important than the rest of the application information. It can add something—like a cherry on top of an ice cream sundae—but it's not going to determine the success of your application.

Quick Recap

1. Be capable of describing as much of the grant request as possible in 100 words or fewer. This will help you write the summary as well as define the specifics of your project.
2. Make sure the title of your project gives information about your request—it will be the grant reviewer's first impression of your application.

3

Parts of a Grant Application

Organizational Information

All grant applications ask for at least some organizational information. They want to know who will do the activity, who will assist, and who will benefit. This part of the grant proposal may also ask about your school's demographics—things like your school's percentage of English language learners or the free or reduced-price lunch percentage. Here are some ways various grant applications ask for organizational information:

- **Student demographics?**
- **Please describe the student population served by your school.**
- **In 100 words or less, briefly describe the geographic location and composition of the population your organization serves.**

Many times, you can respond to these questions with data. If the application asks for the information in a narrative answer, be specific. For example, it's not very helpful to say "many" of the students in your "not very big" school are from "high-poverty" families. Instead, say 70% of the 400 students in your

K-5 school come from families with incomes limited enough to qualify for free or reduced-price lunch. Most grant applications limit the length of your responses. Using specific details gives the reader more information in fewer words, and you're making every word count!

Any grant application you complete in the future will be that much easier once you learn the following important facts and figures about your school:

1. Your school's free or reduced-price lunch percentage (a commonly used proxy for the percentage of economically disadvantaged students in your school).
2. Your school's total enrollment and grade levels.
3. Your school's ethnic breakdown (These first three pieces of information are available through the National Center for Education Statistics at https://nces.ed.gov).
4. Facts about special populations in your school, such as English language learners, special education students, etc. These populations can be quite diverse, so a simple percentage doesn't tell the whole story. For example, with English language learners, it would be helpful to know the languages they speak and in which grade levels they are studying. I used the distribution of my school's ELL population to good effect in an NEA Foundation Learning and Leadership grant for training our school's teachers. ELL students were much more heavily distributed in the lower grades; pointing this fact out easily justified a grant request to send one of our school's kindergarten teachers to a train the trainer conference on teaching reading to English language learners.
5. Your school's Tax ID number or Employer Identification Number (EIN). This will be listed on the last W-2 you received from your employer at income tax time. Anybody in your district's finance office will also know.
6. Your school's recent test score data. You should already know your own students' test scores, but check with your principal or data manager for historical data on your students or for data on other students in your school. Much

test score and demographic information is also probably available to the public on your state's department of education website. For example, on www.mischooldata.org, my state's website for education data about Michigan schools, I noticed one of the elementary schools in my district had a high gender achievement gap in reading—17% more boys in the bottom 30% on state assessments, compared to an average of 7% more boys at the other elementary schools in the district. I don't teach at that school, so I don't have any explanations for this, but I've already got some great persuasive data that school's teachers could use to show need in grant applications to fund special programs such as an after-school reading and running program that would seek to engage boys. Compare your school's test scores and demographic data to other schools too. Doing so will not only help you find facts and figures that justify your present grant application, but it may also help you find an entirely new, even more compelling need that fits another grant program.

7. Any big changes in the above numbers. For example, Nebraska's state department of education website told me the percentage of English language learners in the elementary school in my small hometown recently increased by 6%, going from 10% to 16% of the student population in five years, while the percentage of ELL students statewide remained steady. If I were a teacher in this elementary school, I could use this piece of data effectively in a grant application aimed at helping English language learners. My own school in Michigan has a 54% free or reduced-price lunch percentage, but what's telling is it has nearly doubled in the last ten years. Noting the changes in numbers is sometimes even more significant than the numbers themselves. Use data like this about your own students to prove a point in your grant application.

Learning all this information about your school and students will also make you a more informed teacher. Too often, individual educators are so busy teaching their own students (the "trees") they fail to learn much about the wider environment, their school (the "forest"). At a conference once, I was talking with a teacher from another state and was surprised at how much he seemed to know about his school and how easily he was able to answer all my questions. When I commented on this, he told me it was because he wrote lots of grant applications!

A good side effect of gathering data to support your proposal is it will make it easy to be specific. You'll be less likely to use platitudes. If I had a dollar for every time teachers described their students as "amazing" on www.donorschoose.org, the crowdfunding website for teachers, I'd be a very rich teacher myself and could start up my own grant programs. Instead of using vague phrases like "amazing," "awesome," or "fabulous," give the reader concrete evidence. For example, in Figure 3.1, 3rd and 4th grade English language learners responded to an application question about why they should be selected for a free field trip grant award through the Kids to Parks Day school contest (www.parktrust.org). Stephanie, Mary, and Jolien didn't need to say they were "amazing" or "hard working." Instead, they said they came to school early every morning for 45 minutes to study English. They didn't need to say many students in their school were disadvantaged; instead, they polled their group members and noted in their application that nobody in their group had been to Stony Creek Park. This kind of concrete evidence is much more informative than vague platitudes.

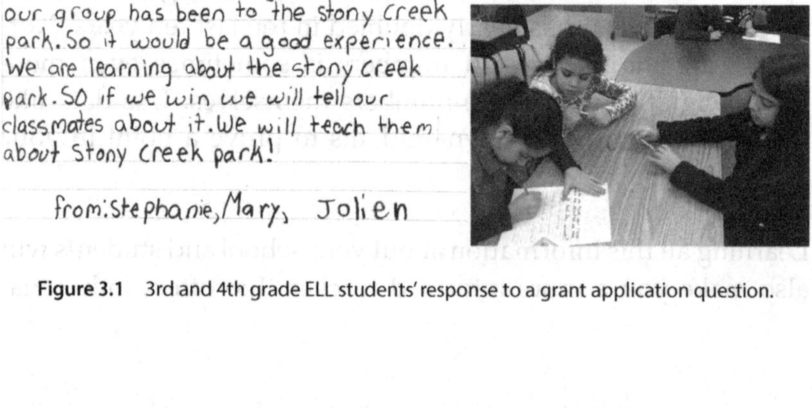

We should be selected because
we come to school early every day for
45 minutes to study English. Nobody in
our group has been to the stony creek
park. So it would be a good experience.
We are learning about the stony creek
park. So if we win we will tell our
classmates about it. We will teach them
about Stony Creek park!

from: Stephanie, Mary, Jolien

Figure 3.1 3rd and 4th grade ELL students' response to a grant application question.

Here is information about my school's demographics I submitted with a grant application for an arts project with our local symphony orchestra:

> Susick Elementary is a K-5 public school in the northern suburbs of metro Detroit. We are the only school in our district, Warren Consolidated Schools, in Oakland County; the rest of our district's schools are in Macomb County. The table below is a breakdown of Susick student ethnicities:
>
> White – 74%
> Black – 7%
> Hispanic – 5%
> Asian – 12%
> Two or more races – 2%
>
> Nearly 80% of Susick students are white, non-Hispanic, but this masks a great amount of diversity because many of our students come from Middle Eastern backgrounds, but are classified as white, non-Hispanic. Fifty percent of our students come from homes where a language other than English is spoken; 25% of our students are still English language learners. Arabic/ Chaldean are the most commonly spoken languages, but we have many others; at last count, some 28 different languages were spoken in Susick homes! According to Public School Review (www.publicschoolreview.com).
>
> Susick has a diversity index higher than the state average. We have anecdotal evidence of this as well. Several recent visitors to our school have complimented us by saying the student body looked like "a mini-United Nations." Susick students themselves are aware of this and proud of it. When a group of students met with State Representative Martin Howrylak and State Senator Marty Knollenberg last year, nearly all the children told the legislators they liked going to school with so many different kinds of classmates. We have a little bit of everything at Susick Elementary, and everyone sees this as a real strength!

Notice how I combined data with anecdotal evidence to make a point about my school's diversity. I tried to be as specific as possible, but one of the grant reviewers still mentioned during the live webcast grant review that she couldn't understand why we had such a high English language learner population with nearly 80% white students. Of course, she was mistakenly assuming English language learners are Hispanic, but the majority of the English language learners in my school speak Arabic and/or Chaldean. We ultimately got the grant funding, so the reviewer's comment was simply an observation, not something that reduced the application's point total. Still, this comment pointed out to me the importance of spelling everything out clearly. What is obvious to you may not be so obvious to an outside reader.

Quick Recap

1. Learn as much as you can about your students and your school. It will pay off when writing grant applications.
2. Be specific. Avoid vague terms like "many" or "most" and useless adjectives like "amazing" or "awesome."

References

Michigan's Center for Educational Performance and Information (n.d.). *Grades 3–8 Assessments for Macomb ISD, Warren Consolidated Schools, Susick Elementary (2014–15)*. Retrieved from www.mischooldata.org/DistrictSchoolProfiles/AssessmentResults/AssessmentGradesPerformance.aspx

National Center for Education Statistics (n.d.). *CCD Public school data 2014–2015, 2015–2016 school years*. Retrieved from https://nces.ed.gov/ccd/schoolsearch/

National Park Trust. Kids to Parks Day school contest (n.d.). Retrieved from www.parktrust.org/kids-to-parks-day/school-contest/

Nebraska Education Profile (n.d.). *2015–2016 Education Profile for Benkelman Elementary School*. Retrieved from http://nep.education.ne.gov

Public School Review (n.d.). *Susick Elementary School*. Retrieved from https://www.publicschoolreview.com/susick-elementary-school-profile

4

Parts of a Grant Application

Statement of Need

All grant proposals expect a statement of need, although it may not be stated directly as a question in the grant application. The need may or may not be financial; it may also be a need to solve a problem or a need to address an opportunity. Some applications will want you to prove economic need by requesting the percentage of students in your school who come from families with incomes limited enough to qualify for free or reduced-price lunch rates. In fact, some grant programs may restrict applications to schools with a free or reduced-price lunch rate above a certain percentage; others may say they give preference to high-poverty schools. On the other hand, other programs tell applicants they assume everybody has financial need, and you shouldn't focus on that. Read the application directions carefully. The following sample questions from grant applications illustrate how this statement of need can be phrased differently:

- **Is there a student demand for this activity?**
- **How will your project supplement and enhance your curriculum?**
- **Please explain why your project is needed. Tell us facts, figures, and details about the issue that you have learned from experts or from your research.**

Think of ways you might be able to use facts, figures, and examples from your particular school situation to show need. For example, I submitted a grant application for an arts project with our local symphony orchestra just two years after submitting an application for the very same project. Both requests were successful. How did I explain the need so soon after the first project? It was simple—my school has a transient student population. Less than 20% of the students who start as kindergarteners at my school remain until 5th grade; in fact, nearly half are gone by 2nd grade and replaced by new students. In addition, in the year I applied for the second time, our school's attendance area boundaries had been redrawn, so we had added over 80 new students from other attendance areas. Using this data, it was easy to show why a second program with the local orchestra was needed just two years after the first program—the musicians would be playing to a nearly brand-new audience! Once you've gathered demographic information about your school, start thinking about how you can use this information as I did to show need for your grant request.

Here's an excerpt showing need from a state-funded arts in education residency grant application:

> Susick Elementary students have acceptable improvement and achievement averages on the MEAP (Michigan Education Assessment Program) tests that are given to 3rd, 4th, and 5th graders every year. Our biggest challenge is narrowing the gap in student achievement between our highest and lowest performing students. This past year, our gap placed us in the bottom 10% of Michigan schools, thus designating us as a "focus" school. Part of our plan to narrow this gap is to facilitate more integration of all our curriculum areas and to make learning activities authentic, relevant, and tangible. We feel our proposed Arts in Education Residency with Michigan Opera Theatre will provide just this kind of experience and result in increased student achievement.

Here, the case wasn't being made to show financial need. In fact, this grant program's application didn't even ask for a school's free or reduced-price lunch percentage. Instead, another, just as compelling need was outlined in the grant application—the need to close a school's achievement gap and how the proposed grant-funded activity would do that.

This example is from a much smaller, but successful grant application for a 4th grade service-learning project at a local park:

How does the volunteer project address a critical community need?

Several years ago, plummeting property values led to widespread budget troubles for the city of Troy; the Lloyd A. Stage Nature Center was forced to close after a proposal for an additional tax to support the Center was voted down. Fortunately, after several months, the Nature Center reopened as a nonprofit entity, but its hours are limited, and it is heavily dependent on volunteers and donations. The 4th grade students at Susick were very interested in learning about the story behind the Nature Center, and they are eager to help the park and lobby the City Council on its behalf. One of the main reasons the tax proposal for the Nature Center was rejected in the first place was because many voters weren't aware of the Nature Center and its importance to the community. Doing volunteer cleanup work will give students first-hand experience with this park and build future citizen advocates for it.

This grant application excerpt shows that sometimes the need isn't about the students at all. With support from grant funds, they can be the ones solving a problem or meeting a community need—in this case, the need to clean up a local park and advocate for its continued operation. This example also shows your answers don't necessarily need to be long, just complete. They will be if you respond to every single question that's asked on an application.

Here is another example showing need in an excerpt from a successful grant application for a Learning and Leadership professional development grant from the National Education

Association Foundation. The application requested professional development funding for the district's English language acquisition teachers to learn how to interpret student growth data from the WIDA, the state's annual test of English language proficiency:

What is the need for this professional development? How did you and your colleagues assess the need? Please define need in terms of both student need and professional need by the applicant(s).

This professional development is clearly needed. Our district is telling us that ordering these expected growth reports is outside their budget, but one of the best ways we can use this WIDA data is to look at expected growth. Teachers could individually log into the WIDA website and access the grade level charts to use with each individual student's growth data, but this is a very labor-intensive practice, especially for schools with many ELL students. It's much more efficient to order the expected growth reports for all ELL students, which we can then use to plan our instruction for the coming year.

This past year, our district scheduled *two* opportunities for us to learn about WIDA growth data, but each time, it was cancelled due to time/budget constraints. Our district's teachers need the professional development time provided by this project because we need to teach smarter, not just harder. We're also tired of our central administration putting off this much-needed professional development. An NEA Learning and Leadership grant will allow us to make the training happen and even better, let us control how it's delivered.

We assessed the need for this professional development by looking at the WIDA growth data from last year. Several key points were clear. Teachers were often worried about "low" ELL students when these very same students had growth percentiles rates of over 50%! Clearly, the teachers were being too hard on their students and themselves. Another point was that ELL students at the middle and high school levels weren't performing as well as students at the elementary level. Looking at the growth data will help secondary teachers better understand this. Our district's general education teachers are working hard; we just need to help them work smart.

This application wrote itself. It was very easy for me to make my case to the NEA Learning and Leadership grant reviewers for professional development we teachers could control because my district hadn't followed through on planned professional development for English language acquisition teachers in the past. All I had to do for a successful grant application was point out this fact. The take-away lesson here is to consider your daily teaching frustrations as great ways to gather evidence for grant writing. Can't get what you need? Document it in a grant application! Having a clearly-defined need and being able to show evidence of it will also result in a stronger application that's more likely to be successful. A colleague who has received several grant awards once told me that it seemed her applications were successful when she really, really needed what she was requesting. She obviously was able to show evidence that supported her need—after all, that's why she got the grant awards—but she has a point. For example, if you're a high school science teacher looking at a $1,000 grant announcement and thinking, "Hey this is too good to pass up—guess I'll apply to buy a telescope," that's not enough. A successful grant application is inevitably driven by the need, not the grant announcement. In the same way students produce better writing when they have an authentic reason to write, you'll inevitably produce a better grant application when you have a real need.

Quick Recap

1. You're writing the grant application in the first place, so it's obvious you have financial need. Don't stop there.
2. Think of other kinds of need, such as the need to solve a specific school or community problem.

5

Parts of a Grant Application

Objectives

This section of the grant application is where you get a chance to tell the grant funder what will change after the project is completed. What will the students know then that they don't know now? What will they be able to do then that they can't do now? Will the students create something tangible? Your objectives need to also address curriculum standards and show how the proposed activity will further student learning. Grant funders want to make as much impact with their limited budgets as they can; if your application isn't tightly connected to standards, it's less likely to be funded. Don't be like the educator on www.donorschoose.org, a crowdfunding website for teachers, who was requesting over $800 for a field trip to a water park as a way to celebrate the end of the school year. Even if the teacher were fortunate enough to get the project funded, I'd say using the funds for an activity that's not directly linked to curriculum isn't the best use of the donor's money or goodwill. Tie your project idea to what your students are studying; it will make a better grant application, and it will also result in more student learning.

Sometimes, the application will explicitly tell you to avoid word-for-word objectives and to not write the standards out directly, as in these example questions:

- **State in general terms the curriculum or state standards by which the project activities are driven. Do not include full descriptions of state standards.**
- **How will this project be integrated into the curriculum or day-to-day activities of your organization?**
- **Which curricular content area(s) does your program address? Please select all that apply.**

Other applications will want more detailed information:

> **List at least two specific skills, behaviors, or new knowledge students will gain from this project.**

Again, read the directions carefully. If you're having a hard time articulating the skills and knowledge you want students to gain from your proposed activity, then you're probably not ready to apply for a grant to support it.

This example describes the goals and objectives from a grant application through the Michigan Council for Arts and Cultural Affairs for an arts in education residency my school was proposing to do with Michigan Opera Theatre:

> Creating an original opera is by its very nature an interdisciplinary activity. That's why the opera experience we are planning can easily be linked to core curriculum standards. Students will be challenged to create an opera from a story line out of their textbooks. Michigan's Common Core State Standards emphasize integrated, deep, extensive learning, not learning that is a mile wide and an inch deep. The curriculum for this residency will address the following Michigan Common Core State Standards:
>
> - CCSS.ELA-Literacy.RL5.7 Analyze how visual and multimedia elements contribute to the meaning, tone, or beauty of a text.
> - CCSS.ELA-Literacy.CCRA.R.4 Produce clear and coherent writing in which the development, organization, and style are appropriate to task, purpose, and audience.

- CCSS.ELA-Literacy.CCRA.L.3 Analyze how and why individuals, events, and ideas develop and interact over the course of a text.
- CCSS.ELA-Literacy.CCRA.L.4 Interpret words and phrases as they are used in a text, including determining technical, connotative, and figurative meanings, and analyze how specific word choices shape meaning or tone.

This application was to a state-funded grant program, so the guidelines wanted applicants to show how the proposed project "advanced Michigan content standards." That's why the curriculum objectives were clearly spelled out.

A much less complicated Target Field Trip grant application provides yet another example. This requested the applicant describe the proposed field trip's activities, as well as its objectives, in just 2,000 characters, or approximately 250–300 words:

Describe the field trip you would like to plan for your students.

What's the objective of the trip? Why is it important?
The 2nd grade teachers at Susick Elementary would like to take our students on a field trip to the Michigan Sea Life Aquarium, in Auburn Hills, Michigan. The objective of this outing is to introduce our students to this newly opened museum in our area and to teach them about organisms living in various water habitats. We will use this tour of the Michigan Sea Life Aquarium as the culmination of a thematic reading unit based on sea life. Using thematic units to integrate several different subject areas helps all students, but research shows thematic instruction especially helps English language learners, who make up over half of the students in our 2nd grade. This sea life unit and field trip will do just that. It will also help us meet many of our state's recently adopted Common Core State Standards for English language arts. When we return to school, students will choose a sea life creature they saw at the Sea Life Aquarium, read several different

nonfiction sources about it, and combine this information with what they learned on their field trip to write a short research paper, thus meeting another Common Core State Standard for English language arts.

Working with a limited number of characters, I couldn't completely spell out the specific curriculum objectives as I had in the much longer narrative for the opera residency. The fact that the response was limited to 2,000 characters, however, indicated that I wasn't expected to. I did, however, outline what we wanted the students to be able to do as a result of the field trip. Looking at this response now, I'd have added something about how Michigan's recently adopted Common Core State Standards especially emphasize reading and writing about nonfiction. I didn't make that clear. You'll find, too, you can see opportunities for revision in nearly every grant application you revisit. That's why it's so beneficial to submit your great idea to several grant programs—and to keep revising and submitting it, even after it's rejected. You'll write a better and better application!

Quick Recap

1. Tie your grant request to curriculum standards. You do this every day in your teaching; just make sure it's obvious in your application.
2. Revise and resubmit an unsuccessful application—you'll get better!

6

Parts of a Grant Application

Project Activities

The project activities section is the nuts and bolts part of the grant application that gives you a chance to show you've really thought out how you will implement the grant. The following questions are examples of how different applications might request this information:

- **How long will the program last?**
- **Describe sequentially what the students will do during the project.**
- **Methods for achieving objectives.**

This project timeline was used to describe the planned activities for a six-month arts in education residency grant program. The application guidelines for this program specifically requested a timeline, probably because the residency was a lengthy project with lots of moving parts and players. Still, the timeline format is an efficient one that could be adapted for smaller projects as well:

Project Timeline for Our Proposed Arts in Education Residency:

- January – Susick classroom teachers do basic orientation to opera before assembly.
- Mid-January – Michigan Opera Theatre (MOT) visits Susick Elementary to perform *The Pied Piper of Hamelin* for the whole school. This will serve as background building, an introduction to story-telling through opera.
- Friday, January 30 – Classroom teachers and other staff meet with project director from MOT for preliminary session and orientation to opera-creating process.
- February 2015 – One or more MOT teaching artists will be involved with each of the following scheduled sessions, with the exception of the April 24 trip to the opera.
- Friday, February 6 – Create story line.
- Friday, February 13 – Finalize story line; begin writing libretto.
- Friday, February 27 – Continue writing libretto.
- Friday, March 6 – Begin composing music.
- Friday, March 13 – Continue with music.
- Friday, March 20 – Casting.
- Friday, March 27 – Set design.
- Thursday, April 2 – Set design.
- Friday, April 17 – Practice in groups.
- Thursday, April 21 – Practice in groups.
- Friday, April 24 – Attend performance of *The Very Last Green Thing* by the Michigan Opera Theatre Children's Chorus.
- Friday, May 1 – Practice in groups.
- Friday, May 8 – Final rehearsals.
- Friday, May 15 – Final rehearsals.
- Thursday, May 21 – Presentation at Susick Talent Show.
- Friday, May 22 – Opera road show at Cherrywood Nursing and Living Center.
- 2015–2016 school year and beyond – Teachers involved with residency will begin helping other classes create their own operas!

It may seem onerous to include so much advance planning in the application, especially because you don't even know if you're going to get the funding to make the project possible. Careful planning now, though, will pay off later if you're fortunate enough to get a grant award. The detailed planning shown in this timeline came in very handy when grant award announcements were delayed, and we got word we'd received funding just one month before the scheduled start of the project. We didn't have to make many changes to the planned activities, either, probably because we had done so much planning up front.

Be sure your activities start *after* the grant awards are announced. Knowing how long it often is between an application deadline and the grant award notification, not to mention the additional time it takes to actually receive the funds, it's easy to see why applicants might be tempted to use grant money retroactively. There are two things wrong with this strategy, however. First, many different grant application guidelines remind applicants this isn't possible, and second, it's just not a good idea to start a program unless you're sure all of it will be funded. What if the grant application isn't successful?

Here is another example showing scheduled project activities from a successful grant application for a school-wide literacy project involving a field trip to a local theater to see *Shrek The Musical JR*. This example frames the activities as ways to achieve the program objectives, each activity linked to an objective listed earlier in the application. Note how specific activities were planned both before the field trip and after the field trip:

Methods for Achieving Objectives:

We will achieve our objectives through the following activities:

- Students, depending on their grade level, will read and/or listen to *Shrek* by William Steig. Students will learn the valuable lessons this story imparts.
- Students will learn selected songs from *Shrek JR.*, thus building background knowledge before attending Warren Civic Theatre's musical production of this story.

Singing the songs will develop reading fluency and integrate the experience with music, another content area.

- Upper elementary students will read the script from *Shrek JR*. This will help build background knowledge, teach basic theater concepts, and introduce them to a new genre.
- Greg Trzaskoma of Warren Civic Theatre will speak to lower elementary and upper elementary groups about producing *Shrek JR*. He'll discuss basic theater concepts and show students examples of costumes, sets, and props from the production. His visit before the play will also build background knowledge for the students.
- Susick Elementary's entire student body will attend Warren Civic Theatre's youth production of *Shrek JR*.
- Follow-up back at Susick will include writing reviews of the musical and thank you notes. Students will also compare and contrast the different versions of *Shrek* they've seen and read.

Once you have defined the objectives and planned the activities to meet the objectives, it's time to evaluate whether the objectives have been met. Chapter 7 tells you how to do this.

Quick Recap

1. Have a clear plan for what your students will do during the grant-funded activity.
2. Thorough planning beforehand results in a better application. It will also save you time during implementation should the project get funded.

7

Parts of a Grant Application

Evaluation Plan

The evaluation plan shows how you'll measure the outcomes of the grant activities. You've already outlined your project's objectives; now you need to show your plan to assess how well you meet them. Here are some sample questions from various grant applications that ask for this kind of information:

- **How are the outcomes of the project measureable?**
- **Describe the method you will use to determine if the objectives have been realized by your students.**
- **How will you evaluate the effectiveness of your project?**

The evaluation plan doesn't always have to include hard data like test scores; it can also use anecdotes, student quotes, opinion surveys, etc. Here's a description of a quick random sample survey of our school's student body that was taken after a 4th grade science opera that was produced during a grant-funded arts in education residency with Michigan Opera Theatre. The opera was about the three states of matter, a concept 4th graders were studying in science. The survey was conducted to determine the effectiveness of the project, i.e. whether the audience learned something about this topic by attending the opera:

> The science opera from the residency taught everyone about the three states of matter, not just the 4th grade performers. In a random survey of 40 students in grades K-3 who were asked one week later, "What were the three states of matter the 4th graders were singing about in the opera?", 75% of the students were able to respond unprompted, "Solids, liquids, and gases." This is remarkable because these young students hadn't studied this topic yet, and the sample included English language learners and special education students. Even now, the opera is being used as an educational video in science classes.

This information was included in the grant's final report, although it would have been even better if a random sample survey had also been taken before the science opera. This was done for the next arts in education residency our school participated in, a good example of how one gets better at this with experience.

In some cases, the success of a project can be evaluated by whether something tangible was created. Figure 7.1 documents

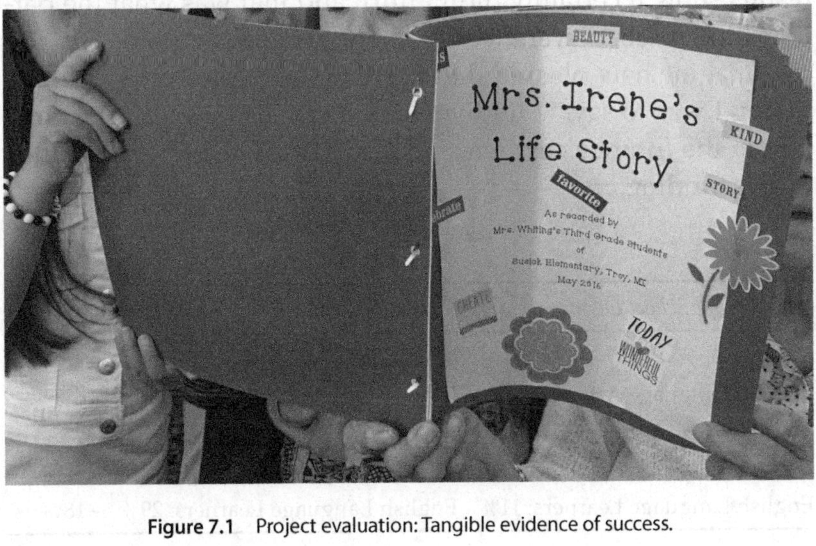

Figure 7.1 Project evaluation: Tangible evidence of success.

evidence of the success of a life story project with residents of a nearby senior living facility. The objective of the grant-funded activity was for 3rd grade students to interview and write the life stories of the residents. The photo nicely proves the project's objective was met as the students share their writing with their senior friends, but it still preserves everyone's privacy.

Table 7.1 shows an evaluation example from the opera residency's final grant report. Our school's principal made this chart using publicly available data from www.mischooldata.org to give our school's teachers some context to our students' test scores. It compares Susick's passing percentages on the M-STEP, Michigan's annual test of English language arts and math given in grades 3-5, to the passing percentages in a neighboring district that is considered more desirable than our school district. It's where many of our students move when their families become more prosperous and buy homes. Note how Susick Elementary had much higher percentages of ELL students and economically disadvantaged (ED) students than the neighboring school district did, yet our 4th grade, the opera grade, had higher passing percentages than the 4th grade in the neighboring, more desirable district. Of course, I couldn't say the grant-funded opera activity led to our school's 4th graders performing better than the 4th graders in the more desirable school district, but these results show it certainly didn't hurt, and that was what the participating teachers were worried about before the residency. You can imagine how pleased they were to see these scores and how happy I was to say, "I told you so!" I can also use this information in the future as evidence to justify the need for other kinds of arts funding.

Table 7.1

Neighboring School District	*Susick Elementary*	*Difference*
4th Grade	4th Grade	
English Language Arts: 50%	English Language Arts: 56%	+6%
Math: 48%	Math: 57%	+9%
Economically Disadvantaged: 33%	Economically Disadvantaged: 57%	+24%
English Language Learners: 11%	English Language Learners: 29%	+18%

These questions from a Target Field Trip grant application comprise one half of the entire application. Although the first two questions seem to be asking for statements of need, the last question directly asks about project evaluation:

> **Benefits of Proposed Field Trip**
>
> **How will students benefit directly from the proposed field trip? How will the experience benefit your curriculum? How will you measure student learning as it directly results from the trip? Please limit your response to 2,000 characters.**

Notice how the following response from a successful application addresses *each* question in three separate paragraphs, with each question stem repeated in the response. For a longer narrative, I might have answered each question with a separate section heading:

Benefits of Proposed Field Trip

Our proposed field trip will directly benefit all our students by showing them many different kinds of sea life and teaching them about their habitats. The trip will also serve as a valuable introduction to a new attraction in our community. This is especially important for the 50% of our students who are English language learners and who typically live in very small wotlds.

This field trip experience will benefit our curriculum because it will introduce our students to an important curricular theme, sea life, through nonfiction.

We will measure student learning by assessing how well our students can complete a writing project that integrates what they previously read about sea life with what they learned on their field trip to the Aquarium. Being able to gather information from several different sources and put it into writing is an important, higher level thinking skill and a Common Core State Standard for English language arts. If our students can do this, our goal for this field trip will be achieved. A final way we can measure the success of our trip is to determine if some of our students return to the Michigan Sea Life Aquarium with their parents. About 55% of our students come from homes with incomes low enough to qualify for free or reduced-price lunches; they lack the enriching experiences that children from more advantaged backgrounds have. We're hoping that an enjoyable experience at the Michigan Sea Life Aquarium will encourage our students to share what they've learned with the adults in their homes, maybe even resulting in a return visit to the Aquarium with their families.

Posing multiple questions for applicants to answer in a single response can cause problems because it's easy to overlook answering one or more of the questions. Tying your responses closely to the questions makes your application much easier for grant reviewers to read and understand. They most likely are using a rubric to evaluate how well you answer each question in the application. Organizing your answers so you clearly respond to each question reminds reviewers you've addressed *every question*. That will result in more points being awarded on the rubric.

Here is an excerpt from a successful application to a now-defunct Target Arts in the Schools grant program. The application requested funding for a professional puppet play to be performed for our school's lower elementary students with a puppet-making workshop afterwards. The section titled "Measurement" asked two key questions. The first one referenced anticipated outcomes—in other words, objectives:

What are the anticipated outcomes of the project/ program?

1. Students will be able to retell the familiar folk tale of *The Gingerbread Man*.
2. We anticipate that after watching the puppet performance of *Kolobok*, the Russian version of *The Gingerbread Man*, the students will be able to point out differences and similarities between the play and other versions of the folk tale the students studied.

3. Students will successfully make a puppet of their own in the puppet-making workshop after the performance.
4. Students will use the puppets they've made to do their own simple version of *The Gingerbread Man*.

The second question asked how the outcomes would be evaluated:

> **What key metrics do you plan on collecting to determine if the outcomes have been achieved?**

The project will be deemed successful if students can achieve the following outcomes:

1. Retell the story of *The Gingerbread Man*.
2. Point out the differences in the play they see and the other versions of *The Gingerbread Man* they've studied.
3. Make puppets of their own.
4. Stage a puppet show of their own.

Notice how each numbered outcome is linked to its measurement. This made it easier to write and easier for a grant reviewer to score as well.

Quick Recap

1. Use multiple methods to evaluate objectives—assessments, projects completed, anecdotes, random sample surveys, etc.
2. Consider how you'll evaluate each of your project's objectives and clearly show this in your application.

Reference

Michigan's Center for Educational Performance and Information (n.d.). *Grades 3–8 Assessments for Macomb ISD, Warren Consolidated Schools, Susick Elementary (2014–15)*. Retrieved from www.mischooldata.org/DistrictSchoolProfiles/AssessmentResults/AssessmentGradesPerformance.aspx

8

Parts of a Grant Application

Budget and Supplemental Material

This last part of a typical grant proposal includes both the required budget as well as extra information, if it's allowed, such as past publicity notices, participant biographies, letters of support, etc. Here are ways various grant applications have requested this information:

- **Who will be involved in this program?**
- **Please identify the costs of the project by itemizing what you will buy with the funds.**

If you have a choice, it's always better to not have grant money go to you individually; in other words, have your school or district be the fiscal agent, not you. That way, you won't experience any income tax consequences. If it goes to your district, you'll need to make sure it eventually gets back to your specific school. In many cases, you won't have a choice; some grants will award funds to individual teachers, while others will only award grants to institutions. In the latter case, should you move to a new school, the grant award will not follow you, since it was awarded to your school, not to you individually. A teaching colleague and

I found this out the hard way. He taught music at two different schools in our district. Together, we applied for and received a $2,000 Target Arts in the Schools grant (since discontinued) to implement a project with our local symphony orchestra at the school where we both taught. The next year, I helped him apply for a Target Arts grant to do a similar project at the other school where he taught. The good news was the grant application was successful; the bad news was he was transferred to a different school in the district the next year. Unfortunately, the Target Arts grant was awarded to the school, not the teacher, so the project couldn't follow him to his new school. Therefore, a new music teacher implemented a grant project she had no previous knowledge of and might not have wanted in the first place. The core project took place as planned, but the enrichment and extension activities weren't conducted, mainly because the people who carried out the project hadn't even written the grant application. The take-away lesson from this example is to ensure the person who will be implementing the grant will be in a position to do so if it is awarded. Is there a possibility your position will change? If so, this might not be a good year to apply for awards that are attached to a school. It might still be, however, a good year to apply for awards that go to you personally. That was the case with this very same music teacher when I helped him apply for a Kids in Need Foundation grant (www.kinf.org). When he moved to another school the next year, the funds followed him, so he could implement the project there.

I've been told some school districts require teachers to inform their central office about grant applications they are submitting, even if they're just writing small grants for their own classrooms. Even if it's not required, it's a good idea because often, grant money is funneled through a district's central finance office. The finance people for my school district say it's very helpful to know about all grants that are in process so they can remind teachers to file their final reports. They want to avoid the problems that can occur when a teacher goes on summer vacation and forgets to file the final report for the grant project. When the grant program contacts the central office people, they don't know anything about the project, and the grant money has to be returned because the final reports weren't filed. That's the worst-case scenario, and you don't want that outcome. In some cases, a percentage of the award is withheld until the final reports are filed; in other cases, you aren't given the money up front; you need to file for reimbursement with all the appropriate documentation. Programs with these kinds of payment put a premium on final report follow-through. Getting the grant is just the start—you need to file final reports to get the entire award. Even if you're given the entire grant award up front, it's still very important to file final reports. Failing to do so will render you ineligible to apply for future awards. You don't want that outcome, either. In addition to your finance office, it's a good idea to tell others around you about in-process grant applications. Many applications ask for a letter of support, signature, or other evidence of buy-in from your principal or other administrators. Collecting signatures may seem like a hassle, but forcing you to assemble a team of people who not only know about your project but also support it is one way funders are helping you to be successful if you're eventually awarded a grant. Working closely with finance people in your district's central office, then, is necessary—and it's also sound practice. My only caution is to make sure you don't leave the grant writing to people outside the classroom. Even if your district has a full-time grant writer, you as a classroom teacher are still in the best position to apply for smaller classroom awards because you understand your students' needs better.

For me, a typical classroom teacher, the budget is probably the most difficult part of any grant application, maybe because it's a difficult part of my everyday life to manage as well! Your training and experience as a teacher are a great help to you as you plan project activities, determine objectives, make connections to the curriculum, and evaluate the effectiveness of your grant-funded project. You most likely have far less professional preparation for making a budget. It requires you to consider everything—the project activities, the price of the activities, and the justification for the amount of money you are requesting. In a large application, you'll have a chance to explain budget items in the general narrative; there may even be a separate budget narrative required. In smaller grant applications without budget narratives, you'll have to be as specific as possible when describing the line items on the budget spreadsheet. Some programs want your budget to exactly total the amount of the grant award being offered, which I find particularly annoying. Life just isn't that exact. Other applications will allow you to request what you need up to a maximum amount. I have seen some programs that want to be the sole funder of your project, so your costs can't exceed the grant award. Other programs, however, will help fund a project that costs more than the grant award. You'll just have to note in the budget where you're getting the rest of the money.

Read the directions carefully to avoid requesting money for items that aren't allowed. This may also help you determine whether your project idea is best for this grant program. Once, during a webcast grant review, I heard the reviewers discuss an application that was requesting funds for a student field trip to Canada. This was a Michigan-based grant program, so Canada as a destination wasn't very far away, but the rules plainly stated funds for out-of-state travel could not be requested. The grant reviewers summarily dismissed the application. I once served as a reviewer for a grant program that funded instructional materials but not textbooks; several of the applications I read requested money to buy textbooks. Careless budgeting like this wastes everybody's time.

Most application directions will remind applicants to be as accurate as possible when determining costs. It's not good to pad the budget with excessive costs or frivolous items, mainly because it indicates the project won't be implemented well. On the other hand, you need to include everything and be as accurate as possible with costs so you don't come up short. Once, when trying to meet a deadline for a field trip grant application, I guesstimated the cost of park admission based on what it had been several years earlier. After we got the grant award check for the amount I had requested, we discovered, much to my chagrin, that admission costs had increased. The take-away lesson from this is two-fold—determine costs carefully, and don't prepare the application at the last minute, especially the budget!

Figure 8.1 shows a simple budget that was part of a successful Kids to Parks Day free field trip grant program (www.parktrust.org). This program helpfully provided a budget template with

Budget for Park Visit

Students—please complete the brief budget for your park trip

Item	Explanation	Cost
Bus/transportation -contact your bus company for pricing	One very full bus for 6 hours @ $45/ hour = $270. We'll need the bus to stay at the park because it will be driving the students from the Nature Center to the canoe dock and back again. (Stony Creek Metro park is a very big park!)	$270
Park Experience/other fees -canoe rentals, entrance fee, guided tour, or other park fees	Nature Center program 53 students @ $3/student = $159 Voyageur canoe program 4 groups @ $75/group = $300	$459
Stewardship Project -plants, mulch, cleaning supplies, trash bags, vinyl gloves or other supplies	We won't need any supplies to make sure our picnic area is left clean and tidy!	$0
Other -snacks, refreshments, educational materials	Students will bring their own healthy lunches and drinks. Educational materials will be created from readily available school supplies. Students in the before-school program for English language learners will make an orientation video for their classmates.	$0
	Total:	$729

Figure 8.1 Sample budget from a grant application for a field trip. Source: Kids to Parks Day School Contest.

instructions and suggestions for items that might be needed. Even this simple budget, though, required a lot of advance footwork, like finding out what the bus rental cost was and determining how many buses would be needed and for how long. We also needed to call the park to determine the cost of the two student educational programs. This grant program offered awards of up to $1,000, but the students felt we didn't need to request money for any other items. This showed willingness to be good stewards of the grant funds if we were fortunate enough to get the grant, which we did.

Table 8.1 shows an example of the budget from an arts project with our local symphony orchestra group through a state agency, the Michigan Council for Arts and Cultural Affairs.

Table 8.1

Budget–Susick Elementary Classicalpalooza

Income	*Cash*	*In-kind*	*Totals*
Revenue—earned			
Revenue—unearned			
Applicant Cash	$1,440		**$1,440**
In-kind revenue			
Itemized in expense column		$747	**$747**
MCACA Mini-grant request			**$2,060**
TOTAL CASH REVENUE			**$4,247**

Expenses—cash	*Cash*	*In-kind*	*MCACA share*	*Totals*
Employee costs				
18 classroom teachers x 1 hr @ $40/hr.	$720			
Media specialist x 3 hours x $40/hr.	$120			
Project director—15 hours x $40/hr.	$600			**$1,440**
Non-employee costs				
Artists' fees—7 musicians	$1,500		$1,500	**$1,500**
Additional project-related costs				
Rubber bands, deli containers, styrofoam trays, straws	$200		$200	
Bus transportation to Cherrywood Nursing Home for performance	$90		$90	
Susick gym rental—1 assembly @ $150		$150		
Cherrywood resident volunteers to assemble rubber bands, cut straws, and cut cups—10 hrs. @ $23/hr.		$230		
Invitations—450 copies x $.10/copy		$45		
Parent volunteers to collect water bottle mouthpieces, roll tubes for horns, assemble kits—10 hrs@ $23/hr.		$230		
Retired teacher volunteer for instrument-making workshop—4 hrs. @ $23/hr.		$92		
Books to prepare for performance; one book each for 18 classrooms @ $15/book	$270		$270	
				$1,307
Total expenses				**$4,247**

This application was for funding to bring a local mini-orchestra to our school for an assembly, followed up by an instrument-making workshop. Applications for taxpayer-funded grants like this tend to be more complex, budget included. Many such applications ask you to note matching or in-kind funds. This one required applicants to provide matching funds equal to the grant amount requested. Matching funds can be money from your parent-teacher organization or the value of in-kind volunteer time—for example, if you have parent volunteers helping you do some work. It can also be the cash value of the time teachers spend on the project during school hours ("Employee Costs" in the budget) or the cost of gym rental, office staff time, printing costs, etc. Even though your school is providing these items at no direct, extra cost for the project, you can count them as matching funds for your grant request. In this budget, the items listed in the column under "MCACA share" were the actual grant funds being requested. All the other expenses were costs that the school would incur and would count as the match for the grant funds. "Unearned revenue" refers to the value of items or services provided at no cost to the applicant; in other words, it's the value of volunteer work, teacher time, and use of existing facilities listed under "costs." This application didn't use a budget narrative, so I had to be as specific as possible in the line item descriptions.

Some programs want to be the sole funder of your project; other programs don't care, but they want to know where you're getting the rest of the money for your project. Most of the proposals I've written have been funded at 100%, but it's not uncommon to be funded for only a portion of your request; in fact, some applications ask if you would be able to go forward with the project if you didn't get full funding. Prioritize your budget items, at least in your mind, so you can make cuts if need be.

What kinds of supplemental material can be included as attachments or appendices? Application directions will often guide you. You may be given the opportunity to supply more information about people who will be part of the grant project. Here is an example from an application for an arts in education residency with Michigan Opera Theatre. It's a short bio about one of the teaching artists who would be involved in the residency:

Vocal Coach Pette Moore, baritone, served in the United States Army for eight years, during which he served three tours in Iraq. Stationed in Germany, he studied voice privately and performed throughout Europe and the Caribbean. Since returning home to Detroit, Mr. Moore is studying music at Wayne State University and performs frequently with the Michigan Opera Theatre Touring Company and main stage productions. Mr. Moore sang the popular role of Papa Araboolie in last year's production of *The Araboolies of Liberty Street*; Susick students will be delighted to welcome him back to Susick as a vocal coach.

In addition to noting this person's artistic qualifications, I also pointed out Mr. Moore's previous involvement with Susick. This was a way of assuring grant reviewers this person could work successfully with our students. If you don't have these kinds of past connections, you'll write a stronger application after you've established some. In addition to the bios I submitted for the opera people who would participate in the project, I also wrote short bios for the staff members at my school who would be involved. Here is an example of a teacher bio I wrote the next year for another arts in education residency, but this time with PuppetART Theater:

Rikki Mutter is a 4th grade teacher at Susick whose class was the core group for last year's Michigan Opera Theatre residency. She knows first-hand how much these kinds of experiences can benefit students and decrease the achievement gap. She is willing and able to use her opera-making experience to help her new students create a puppet opera.

Notice how I referenced this teacher's past experience with an arts in education residency and her willingness to participate again. The fact that she wanted to use puppets to create an opera, the subject of the previous year's residency, was evidence of the sustainability of the previous year's grant project. Linking projects together like this creates a powerful "virtuous cycle" of sustainability, each experience building on another. It's hard to deny funding to applications that can show this.

For a large project, it's also important to indicate how various roles will be filled if people become unavailable. In fact, the National Education Association Foundation grant application forms, for example, specifically ask primary applicants to designate an alternate who can take over the project in the event the primary applicant can't do it. Even if your application doesn't specifically ask for this information, give it some thought, and clearly spell out what each project *position* entails, so the proposal isn't dependent on specific individuals. Lead times between the application and the actual activity can be long, and in between, people can change jobs, transfer to other schools, or go on leave. Other supplemental information you might include could be press clippings of successful related past projects to serve as evidence your school is capable of carrying out your proposed grant project. Supplemental information might also be letters of support from community partners who will be participating in the project or supporting it in other ways. For example, I contacted our school's Michigan state representative for support of another taxpayer-funded arts in education grant application our school submitted:

> Rep. Howrylak,
>
> Thank you for introducing the joint resolution to amend Michigan's Constitution to establish a non-partisan unicameral legislature. I've lived in five different states, but I was born and raised in Nebraska and still have family and farming interests there. I can tell you that this unique legislative system works! I'm glad you're working to get Michigan voters to consider it.
>
> Also, Susick Elementary applied again for another arts in education residency grant from the Michigan Council for Arts and Cultural Affairs, this time in partnership with PuppetART Theater in Detroit. The past year's residency with Michigan Opera Theatre was so successful that we hope we can involve

even more students this coming year. Grant winners will be announced in September. We would appreciate anything you can do as a state legislator to support Susick's application. We're sure you realize how much Susick students benefit from these tax-supported programs!

Barbara Gottschalk
English language acquisition teacher
Susick Elementary
Troy, MI

I am not this particular legislator's constituent; I only work at a school in his district. Still, notice how I began the email with something we could both agree on, the importance of the bill he had just introduced for consideration in the Michigan House of Representatives. I also referenced previous grant activity we had told him about and that he had supported. Although I didn't specifically ask for one, this legislator's constituent relations assistant drafted a letter of support for our proposed project and even sent it to me to preview. Our school's grant request, which was three times larger than the one in the previous year, was successful. Representative Howrylak had visited our school every year for several years. We also kept him updated through invitations and thank you notes about student activities funded with Michigan tax dollars, so it was easy to contact him about supporting our grant application. This points out the importance of developing long-term relationships with potential grant partners and supporters. Two weeks before the application deadline isn't the time to start doing this. Although I didn't have to do it in this case, it's certainly acceptable to directly ask for letters of support; these can be included as attachments in a larger grant application, if allowed. Just make sure the letters sound authentic. Once, while serving on a grant review panel, I read an application that had letters of support for the project from several very different institutions that were *exactly the same*. Cut and paste jobs like this are obviously not very effective.

Quick Recap

1. Have a contingency plan for the project should your teaching position change.
2. Determine project costs carefully. This will allow you to make an accurate budget that only requests allowable items.
3. It's best if you have previous connections or experience with the people who will be participating in and supporting your project.

Reference

Michigan's Center for Educational Performance and Information (n.d.). *Proficiency percentage for Susick Elementary and Utica Public Schools (2014–15)*. [Table showing 4th grade proficiency rates on ELA and math M-STEPs]. Retrieved from www.mischooldata.org/DistrictSchoolProfiles/AssessmentResults/AssessmentGradesProficiency.aspx

9

Proposal Writing Tips

MONEY

Now that you understand the mechanics of writing a grant application, you're ready to hone your grant idea. Of course, it's important to submit a well-written grant application, but if the project idea you're writing about isn't a good one in the first place, you'll be merely gilding a lily. The next two chapters will give you ten tips for turning your great idea into a successful grant application. To help you remember these tips, I'll use the mnemonic device **MONEY TALKS.** For example, in my own school, because I can obtain grant funding, I've made it possible for my fellow teachers to incorporate more project-based learning, service learning, and the arts into their teaching. These kinds of activities benefit all students, but especially English language learners, the students I support as my school's English language acquisition teacher. That's money talking!

M is for Make Time

"I don't have the time" is the first reason we all give when we can't seem to get something done. For busy teachers, it's a good reason, too, as swamped as they are with the daily demands of their classrooms. I'll admit the learning curve for grant writing is steep in the beginning. You'll spend the most time and effort of all on your first grant application, but after that, it gets easier and faster. As with most things, the more you practice, the better you become. What's really nice is you can start using bits and pieces from past grant applications in future applications. For example, your school's basic demographic information won't change much; you can simply customize it to fit your specific grant request. If I were requesting funds to buy bilingual books for my school's media center, for example, I'd emphasize my school's high percentage of English language learners and the number of different languages spoken in our students' homes. If I were requesting funding for transportation for an after-school program, I'd point out the high percentage of students from families with incomes limited enough to qualify for free or reduced-price lunch (a commonly-used proxy for the percentage of economically disadvantaged students in a school). Information and project requests can be recycled, but be careful to customize each grant request. You don't want to submit an application like the one I once reviewed that was obviously a canned request sent out to multiple organizations—the writer even used the wrong organization's name in the narrative. Oops.

In addition to recycling parts of previous applications, you can also save time by keeping a running list of upcoming application deadlines, with the closest ones at the top of the list. This can help you prioritize what you should be working on at the moment. You should also keep a list of applications you've already submitted. This can help you remember and track down emailed notifications that might have ended up in your spam folder. To help you remember your login and password for online grant applications, write it at the top of the written application you're drafting offline. That will save you time as well. Many grant programs have online grant systems that send you automatic reminders if you've started an application online; these persistent emails as the application deadline approaches are very helpful for procrastinators.

You can also save time by knowing the application guidelines and selection procedures. For example, a local foundation was offering back-to-school grants for individual classrooms and entire schools. I started answering the application questions in a separate document but then reminded myself to take my own advice and read the eligibility requirements and selection process—in other words, the fine print. How surprised I was to learn the winners of these $100 and $1,000 "grants" would be selected randomly from the applications! There's nothing wrong with this, and the program wasn't keeping this fact a secret. Still, the average teacher spending time carefully crafting a 3,000-character response to three different questions would probably assume the winners would be chosen by a review committee. I submitted applications to both the classroom and whole-school program anyway, but I spent absolutely no time writing a particularly thoughtful response to the questions. Why would I when the winners would be chosen at random? I ended up saving myself lots of time by carefully reading the selection procedures. That's why it's important to know and obey the application rules . . .

O is for Obey the Application Rules

This seems like stating the obvious, but every tip sheet I've seen has mentioned this, so it's something many grant-seekers overlook. I once served as a reviewer for a small grant program for teachers; nearly half of the applications I read didn't follow the basic guidelines. The answers to the application questions exceeded the maximum word limit, the requests were for items that weren't allowed, or the programs didn't meet the eligibility requirements. In other words, the grant writers hadn't obeyed the application rules—and these were proposals written by teachers, who, of all people, should understand the importance of rules. They enforce them every day in their classrooms! Staying within the allowed word limit, for example, may not necessarily be a scoring item on the review rubric, so it's not a deal breaker, but failing to follow application rules does indicate an applicant's ability to successfully implement a grant proposal. If applicants can't follow application guidelines, how in the world will they competently implement their grant projects and file required final reports? That is something all grant reviewers will consider and score accordingly on a rubric.

Even though most grant proposals are filed online, the application is often available to download offline. This will give you an overall idea of what's required before starting. It will also allow you to complete your answers to the questions to submit later online. This is necessary if you aren't allowed to save your application online and submit it later. Applications that don't allow you to do this are one annoyance; another annoyance is applications that require you to fully complete one page before proceeding to the next one. One work-around is to just put a letter or two in each box; this will usually allow you to go on to the next page and see all the application questions.

Reading the application rules will help you save time because you won't be filing useless grant applications. A colleague once told me she had submitted an application for a Target Field Trip grant for a fall field trip to the orchard. I wish the Target Field Trip program funded field trips taken in the fall, but unfortunately for my colleague, it didn't. By reading the application rules carefully, she would have saved herself time and avoided disappointment.

The most obvious rule that needs to be noted and then obeyed is the deadline. I've applied to a few grant programs with rolling deadlines, meaning grants were awarded to worthy applications until the funding ran out. If you encounter programs like this, hurry up and submit an application, just like I did! Deadlines are also sometimes extended, which always makes me wonder why. Have reviewers already determined there aren't enough high-quality applications? That's good news if you haven't submitted yet; bad news if you have. I usually assume an extended deadline means the program isn't getting as many applications as anticipated, regardless of quality; that's good news because it means less competition. Nearly all grant applications are now done online or through email, so working right up until the deadline is much easier, but this can also add its own special set of challenges. I once missed the 12:00 *noon* deadline for a grant application because I was waiting to submit the nearly complete application that evening, before what I thought was the 12:00 *midnight* deadline. That left me with a fully prepared application—but unfortunately, for the next year's grant program. Waiting until the last minute to submit an online application also leaves you vulnerable to last-minute technical glitches; trust me, the closer you get to the submission deadline, the more difficulties you're bound to have. This isn't just karma punishing you for being a procrastinator, either. Sometimes, technical glitches can occur when many people just like you are hitting the "submit" button at the last minute on the application's website. Avoid these needless hassles by submitting at least 24 hours before the deadline.

One way to help you follow the rules is to take advantage of all the resources grant programs often offer to applicants. Read the eligibility requirements first; these are usually available online and can help you determine whether you should even apply to begin with. Once you've determined you're eligible, read the application and the application guidelines carefully. You may get more information that helps you make a decision whether to go forward or not. For example, perhaps the application requires several signatures from your supervisor(s), and to do that, they need to create an online account. You're obviously going to need more lead time to complete this kind of application by the deadline than you would need with one that needs only one signature or none at all.

Grant programs sometimes offer webinars to help potential applicants. These are useful; you should attend them or view them later if they're archived and you can't attend at the designated time. Although it's a much larger investment of time, I've also attended useful in-person workshops offered by larger, local grant programs that answered many of my questions. As it is in many such cases, much of the information from specific grant program workshops can be helpful when applying for grants in other contexts, just as educating yourself in general (as you are in reading this book) is useful for specific grant programs. Finally, grant managers are also available to answer applicants' questions during the application period. It's futile to try to curry favor with them—they want all applications to be good ones, including yours. Still, simply because they want all applications to be good ones, they're valuable resources in helping you follow the grant application rules. Some people advise seeking feedback on unsuccessful applications, although I've never been able to get much—reviewers' comments were either vague or unavailable. I've found it much more helpful to be proactive and seek advice before applying.

N is for Never Start New

If you already have something in place, grant funders will be more likely to give money to help you expand your initiative. For example, here's a paragraph from the grant narrative for an arts in education residency describing my school's previous involvement with PuppetART Theater, our partners in the grant application. Note how I emphasized our activities with PuppetART Theater before at Susick Elementary and how we wanted to take it to the next level:

> Susick has a history of successfully hosting artists for assembly/workshop programs. In previous years, we hosted PuppetArt Theater through a Target Arts grant. Our second graders also visited PuppetART Theater last year through a Target Field Trip grant for a performance of *Mouk's Adventures*. A key factor in the success of these programs was that they weren't one-day programs at all—Susick's teachers thoroughly prepared the students and conducted follow-up activities as well. The excitement (and learning!) lasted many weeks. The same thing will occur with a PuppetART arts in education residency.

I used to think programs wanted brand-new ideas that you were trying out for the first time, but I've discovered that's not the case at all. Of course, many applications will ask you how your project idea is new or innovative, but the reviewers understand very little is totally new under the sun. What's better and more reassuring to grant reviewers is when you're trying out a new spin on a project you have experience with already, or maybe you simply want to expand an innovative approach you've already tried out on a small scale. Funders don't mind giving money to people who already have experience successfully implementing grant programs; that past experience is a good indication future grant projects will be successfully carried out. In fact, it's even better to give money to people who have experience implementing projects similar to the one being proposed in the grant application.

I once used a local newspaper article about a grant-funded visit to Susick Elementary by a local orchestra group as a supplemental attachment in a successful grant application for an arts in education residency with PuppetART Theater, a puppet organization. The orchestra project had no direct connection to the project planned with PuppetART Theater, but the point of including this information was to show our school had experience implementing large grant awards, and we could be counted on to implement another grant award with just as much care. It also showed we knew how to promote the award funders through good publicity. Grant funders appreciate getting credit!

E is for Everybody Involved

"If I apply for a grant," a colleague said to me, "I want to keep all the goodies to myself." She was joking, or at least I hope she was, because failing to look beyond her own classroom could actually hurt her grant application. All other things being equal, grant funders are more likely to look favorably on programs that can benefit large numbers of students. This doesn't mean your idea for your own classroom won't be funded, however. In fact, I've seen some grant applications that requested the number of students the proposal would benefit and then proceeded to reassure the applicant that putting down a smaller number wouldn't affect the application negatively. I've also seen applications that warn applicants not to inflate the number of students who will benefit because the grant program doesn't necessarily favor projects for large numbers of students. The best possible compromise, especially if the grant application doesn't specifically mention equally considering programs for both small and large numbers of students, is to show evidence of having tried out your project idea on a small number of students first. Once you're successful in your own classroom, think about how you could expand it to other classrooms or even to the community. You'll be more likely to get funded for a larger number of students later if you've got a track record with your project idea already.

For example, as part of my school's application for an arts in education residency with Michigan Opera Theatre, we budgeted for a performance of *The Pied Piper of Hamelin* for the whole school by Michigan Opera Theatre professionals. The opera included six singing parts for children. The opera people told us that schools almost never had the children sing; they just chose six students who stood on stage. We definitely wanted the six students we chose to participate, so when the opera people came to school to work with the 4th graders on residency activities, they also helped the six 3rd grade students prepare for their roles in *The Pied Piper of Hamelin*. The lucky 3rd graders ended up singing with the MOT professionals in front of the whole school at the performance, a good example of involving everybody. In this case, the main part of the grant activity involved a core group of 4th graders creating and performing an original opera, but it also included a professional performance for the entire school as well as participation opportunities for additional 3rd grade students. That's a good example of involving everybody.

Y is for Youth Input

Youth input may be more difficult with young children, but it's important to show that students, regardless of their grade level, are actively involved in your project's planning and execution. Many programs emphasize this; some even have application questions that directly address it, as in this sample question from a State Farm Good Neighbor Student Achievement grant application:

> **Youth Voice: How will you include intentional opportunities for students to make decisions at all stages of your program?**

We successfully applied for a grant to fund a series of visits by students throughout the school year to a local nursing home. Here is how the question about youth involvement was answered:

> Students will play a part in deciding what they will do every time they visit Cherrywood. They will choose their favorite songs/dances to perform, and each student will choose the book he/she will read. Students will also determine what kinds of things they will write about in their pen friend letters.

This shows that even the very youngest students can make decisions about grant activities. In this case, the application directly asked about it, but even if a question doesn't specifically address it, you should include information on how your students will be involved. It's even better if the students can actually take part in preparing the application. Figure 9.1 shows the answer 3rd grade and 5th grade English language learners crafted to a question on an application to a Kids to Parks Day National School Contest (www.parktrust.org). This particular grant program specifically requested student input, so these English language learners worked in groups, each group answering a different application question. They also wrote the script for a short video to support the written application. Susick Elementary won a free field trip—for the sixth year in a row. Start thinking about how you can get some student input on your grant applications too.

3) How can you leave the park a better place? How can you be a steward for the park?

We are going to leave the park a better place by not making a mess or making animals eat plastic bottle by picking the trash up. We will make this place popular by telling Students to tell their friends and family members about it. We will follow the nature guide's instructions. The water in michigan is important for itself. After we go to Stony creek park we will learn how water important it is for michigan.

By: Ali, Ryan, Jeremiah.

Figure 9.1 Youth Input: Answering a grant application question.

It's one of the best ways to get students reading and writing for a real purpose. Students don't necessarily need to be directly involved in preparing the application, either. If it's allowed, you can use examples from previous student activities to reinforce your application. Figure 9.2 shows a 1st grade English language learner's journal reflection about a grant-funded field trip to a local assisted living facility. It shows the impact of the experience on the student; her teacher told me this little girl was so eager to get all her thoughts down on paper she even wrote during recess! This kind of artifact and anecdote would be useful to include in future grant applications for funding to continue these field trips to the local assisted living facility. That's exactly why I photographed the student's journal and noted the teacher's comment. It's why you should do things like this too. Your students' writing, comments, and photos are useful, if not necessary, for documenting the success of a grant project in a final report, but these items can also be helpful when preparing future grant applications. Your students are your best advocates—use them!

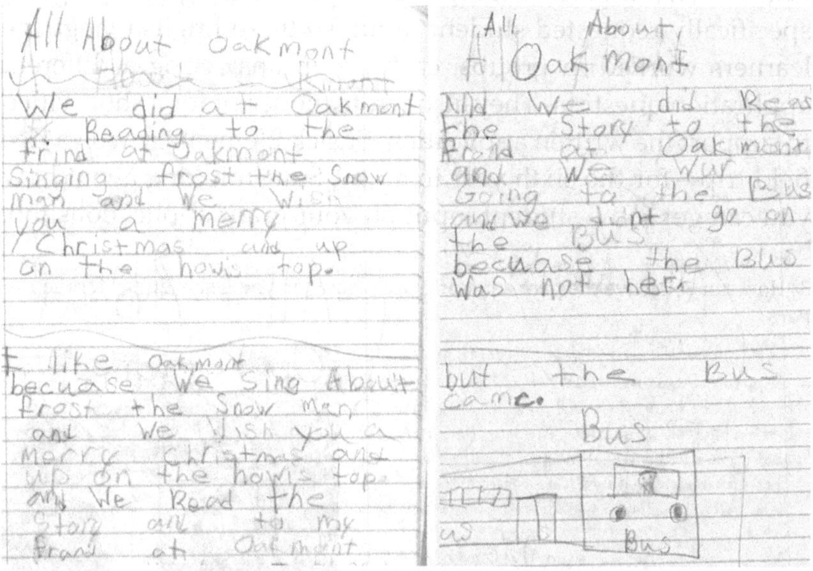

Figure 9.2 Example of a student artifact from a grant-funded experience.

Quick Recap

1. Make the time to submit applications.
2. Obey the application rules—read the guidelines.
3. Build on past experiences—you don't have to be starting something brand-new.
4. Try to get as many students involved in the proposed activity as possible.
5. Think about ways you can involve your students in the application process.

10

Proposal Writing Tips

TALKS

T is for Tell a Story

This is good advice for all persuasive writing, which is actually what a grant application is. For example, I included in an arts in education residency grant application with Michigan Opera Theatre the "story" about seeing how much telling a story through music resonated with English language learners. I included a link to a short video of 1st grade ELL students performing a two-minute opera about *The Gingerbread Man* two years earlier. The story of how opera got started at my school made a good one to tell in the opera residency grant application. For a successful Target Arts in the Schools grant application with our local orchestra, I told the story of how the conductor of the orchestra had visited our school the previous year to talk with the upper elementary students and display his baton collection. I used that visit as evidence of past connections with the orchestra. In a successful Target Field Trip application for a field trip to see a ballet performance of *Aladdin*, I told the story of how nearly all of my newcomer students came from Middle Eastern countries and would be familiar with the tale. Even better, I pointed out how ballet was the perfect kind of performance for beginning English language learners to attend because language wasn't necessary to understand it. In all three of these examples, telling a story basically involved describing the connections in the grant proposal. In the same way you try to provide context when presenting material to your students, a good grant writer will provide context for the application. Telling your story will allow you to give grant reviewers the details of the journey that led to your request. Your proposal shouldn't sound as if you've it drawn out of thin air.

A is for Ask for Action Items

Too often, people apply for grants to buy something ("I want an iPad"), but instead, they should think of their grant request in terms of what they (or better yet, their students) are going to *do* with the money. A good example of how not to look at grant applications is this email I received from a colleague about a grant possibility: "The first one might be good to get us some playground equipment???" It was about a grant program that other schools had used to purchase pedometers for students or yoga mats for gym class, etc. This particular grant was offering schools assistance in building health and wellness *programs*; my colleague was simply looking at it as a way to get stuff. The application *was* relatively simple, but it asked for a detailed action plan on how grant-funded activity would fit into an overall health and wellness school program. Applying for this grant would involve making an integrated plan and assembling a team, ideally headed by the school's physical education teacher; it wouldn't be something a single teacher or parent volunteers could do easily or well. In addition, our school couldn't truly demonstrate compelling need since we had just received new pre-school playground equipment. Starting a grant application this way would doom it to failure.

Nearly all the successful grant applications I've written have been funding requests for things that students can make, do, or experience. Thankfully for my success rate, my personal preference for project-based learning dovetails nicely with what grant programs like to fund—action items, not stuff. Wise parents eventually realize it's what they do with their children that counts, not the things they give them. Grant funders realize this too. It's what students *do* that helps the learning stick. That's why grant programs like to fund projects, not pre-packaged curricula. Even if you do want to buy materials like books, that, in and of itself, wouldn't make an effective grant request. Actually, simply buying books wouldn't in and of itself result in increased student achievement, either. The critical part would be what you planned to do with the books—say, for example, making them a part of a summer bookmobile program or an intergenerational read-aloud program. Start thinking of your grant request in these terms. You'll end up with a better grant application and more student learning too.

L is for Learn What's Funded

I've had proposals rejected by some grant programs—and then accepted by others. I'm convinced the whole process is a lot like a job search. In the same way a job seeker has to find the position that best matches his skill set, you've got to find the right grant program for your idea. It's also important not to "chase the money." All grant applications have eligibility requirements; in fact, many of them have highly targeted eligibility guidelines. For example, some grant programs might be seeking applicants who want to do STEM-related service-learning projects; others might be focusing on after-school programs for under-served middle school students. Grant awards always come with strings; that's a fact of grant life. If you're drastically contorting your project idea to fit the program guidelines, however, it's probably not going to make a strong application—better to find a program that's a good fit.

One of my biggest grant-writing failures was probably the result of a proposal that wasn't the right fit for the program. I applied for a large service-learning grant being offered in Michigan for the first time. I contacted the grant funders to make sure applications from schools would be considered and was assured it was possible, as long as the grant activity period had a summer service component as well as service-learning activities during the academic year. With the help of my principal and input from the various teachers at my school who were interested in teaching in the proposed summer program, we submitted what I thought was a strong application. Uncharacteristically, I was very disappointed when the application was rejected. The $30,000 grant request was for a large amount, at least in my experience, so the planning had involved several people. I was probably disappointed because these people were disappointed too. I felt a bit better, however, when I saw the list of organizations that had received the funding:

- VIP Mentoring in Detroit
- Youth Development Commission in Detroit
- Big Brothers Big Sisters of Greater Flint
- One Love Global in Lansing.

I realized then that our school wasn't a good fit for this grant award. We had been told schools were eligible, but the list of award winners indicated the reviewers were looking for other types of organizations. Often, funders will have lists of previous grant awardees listed on their websites. Even better, they will sometimes have descriptions of past winning projects. Reading through these lists can tell you whether your organization and/or project idea is a good fit. In the case I've just described, the program was new, so I had no information about past award winners to guide me. If such information had been available, I probably would've passed on applying to this grant program. The rejection wasn't a total loss, however. The information gathered to support the application proved useful later in other, successful grant applications.

Here are some sample websites I have used that aggregate various grant sources. Even a casual perusal of the grants available will give you an idea of the hot topics that are getting funding at the moment. As of this writing, it's anything having to do with STEM, service learning, technology needs, school gardens, and other healthy living initiatives, just to name a few:

www.getedfunding.com–This searchable website aggregates grant sources. Sign up to get a weekly e-newsletter with the newest grant programs out. The search engine is moderately useful, but even with the custom search feature, it often returns grant programs that you, as a classroom teacher, won't be eligible for or interested in. Receiving the weekly newsletter, however, will give you a general idea of what's being funded, and that is useful.

www.neafoundation.org–You need to be a member of the National Education Association to apply for their Student Achievement or Learning and Leadership grants, but this website lists other grant programs available to all educators. This list is good because it consists of grant programs aimed at classroom teachers—that would be you! You won't waste time looking at grant programs aimed more at non-profits rather than schools or for large grant programs that would need full-time people to apply for and administer them rather than a single teacher.

www.ysa.org–This is a website for a nonprofit that promotes service learning; it posts available service-learning grants on its home page. Sign up for their weekly newsletter, and you'll get timely information on upcoming grant programs. If you're thinking, "Oh, my idea doesn't involve service learning," well, think again. Is there a way you could seamlessly incorporate some service learning into a class project to qualify?

Once you've worked with other people on applications, they'll start thinking of you whenever they hear about a grant program. You'll also start receiving notices of future grant programs from organizations because you were a past applicant. I'm guessing you're already receiving information about grant programs but just didn't consider applying; hopefully, reading this book will change your mind. Very quickly, you'll find you have more than enough grant sources; a bigger challenge is finding the time to write the applications. Often, I'm asked if local funding sources are better. Based on my experience, I can't say one source is always better than another. I've had great success with national grant programs such as the Target Field Trip program, with an acceptance rate of less than 20%, and limited success with smaller, more local programs. The take-away lesson is to look everywhere to find the right fit!

K is for Keep Trying

"I applied for a Target Field Trip grant when I first started teaching," a colleague once told me, "but I didn't get it, so I just didn't bother again." She was open to taking risks as an enthusiastic new teacher, and she's still an enthusiastic teacher, but that one grant application rejection made her stop trying. That's unfortunate, but I'm guessing my colleague's response is not unusual. Target received over 20,000 applications in 2016 for its Field Trip grant program, so we know the relatively simple application form didn't intimidate at least that many applicants. Still, the National Center for Education Statistics tells us in that same year there were 3.1 *million* K-12 public school teachers in the United States, so that means an infinitesimally small number of people actually applied. Clearly, my colleague who didn't apply again was in the majority, but why? The Target Field Trip grant program has a simple application open to teachers at all grade levels and in all content areas; teachers already have a clearly-defined template for their idea (the field trip); and there are very few final reporting requirements. Even worse, my colleague had already applied, so she'd done all the basic groundwork. It gets easier with each subsequent application. Knowing that, why would anyone stop after applying just once?

I know teachers can deal with rejection; they do it every day. Would teachers stop trying if (just to name a few examples) parents didn't return their phone calls, students didn't turn in their field trip permission slips, or high school students kept skipping class? Of course not! My advice to teachers who have received that all-too-common rejection notice is to use the persistence they bring to other teaching tasks and keep trying.

When a candidate is rejected after a job interview, it often means the interviewers knew more about the job position than the candidate and could determine that the candidate wouldn't be the best fit for the job. It's the same with grant applications; if your application is rejected, it doesn't necessarily mean it's a bad application. It may mean you simply haven't found the right program for it yet. It may also mean your application was the victim of stiff competition. If your grant application isn't successful, you'll often get a notification saying many good applications had to be rejected because there simply wasn't enough money available to fund every worthy project. Believe it; I've been both a paid and volunteer grant reviewer, and from my experience, that's often the case. Here's a list of well-known, national grant programs that have rejected my applications:

- Kids in Need Foundation
- Target Field Trip grant
- Target Arts in the Schools grant (now discontinued)
- State Farm Good Neighbor grant
- NEA Foundation Learning and Leadership grant
- Global Youth Service Day grant.

These same grant programs, however, have also accepted my applications later. This shows you should rework that application and keep trying!

My former principal suggested I track my application activity, so I collected data for six years. You can see in Table 10.1 that except for year four, I was completing about the same num-

Table 10.1

Year	*Number of Applications*	*Success Rate*
1	21	33%
2	22	32%
3	19	53%
4	31	52%
5	21	57%
6	21	62%

ber of applications each year. What the table doesn't show is that I was spending far less time preparing applications in later years. I was more efficient because I had more experience. What the table does show is that my success rate was much higher than it was when I first started. That's because I was a better grant writer, I was a better judge of what was a good fit for an idea, and I was better able to choose grant programs with a higher likelihood of success. I kept track of the dollar amount of funding received for my own curiosity, but that's not noted in the table, mainly because the size of a grant award isn't really relevant. Sometimes, very small awards can make a big impact, especially if they lead to bigger things, and that leads to the next point . . .

S is for Show Sustainability

Grant funders like to know the gift they give will keep on giving. In fact, in some cases they specifically ask about it in the grant application, as in these examples:

- **How will this project continue beyond the grant period? How will you continue sharing the knowledge gained in this project? Describe sharing in relation to your colleagues, students, and administrators.**
- **Can the program be reproduced with little or no cost in the future?**
- **After your project, how will you let others know about the results of your project and involve even more young people to help you expand and keep your project going, so that you can make an even bigger difference?**

Sustainability is easy to show if you intend to buy or make items that can be used for many years to come. For example, I received a grant for materials to make xylophones from metal tubing for students to use in their science studies about sound. Our music teacher later used them in his classes; the students even played them for the residents of a local nursing home. You can be sure

I included a photo of this activity as evidence of the grant's sustainability in the final report. I later used this story and the photos as evidence of sustainability to help this music teacher get another grant to make more metal xylophones to use in his new position as a middle school music teacher in our district.

Training people is another easy way you can build sustainability into your grant request. The excerpt from an arts in education residency grant application with Michigan Opera Theatre shows how I planned for sustainability. The idea was for teachers to learn how it was done and then be able to do it again on their own:

> We want the learning opportunities provided by this residency to extend beyond the grant-funded period. Teachers will gain confidence and experience as they work with MOT artists in guiding Susick students through the creation of their own opera. This confidence and experience, in turn, will serve teachers well as they create simple operas later on a smaller scale, and better yet, show other teachers how it's done.

Sustainability can also be defined as long-term impact on students and teachers. You can show evidence of this kind of sustainability by citing past grant activity in new grant applications. For example, the music teacher who helped implement this arts in education grant project with Michigan Opera Theatre later moved to our district's performing arts middle school, where these kinds of arts-infused projects are done school wide. Because of her experience at Susick, she was able to successfully apply for a similar grant at her new school. This shows the first experience had a strong influence on her, and this sustainability is something I'd mention in future grant applications. Another example of the sustainability of this project was shown when students who were in this opera production as 4th graders came to their 5th grade teacher the next year and proposed doing an original version of *The Wizard of Oz*. They told her they wanted to do "something like the opera." The teacher didn't have the funds to launch a full-scale opera, but her students generated a delightful, original, and entirely student-initiated small-scale production. I applied for another grant with Michigan Opera Theatre the next year, and you can be sure I mentioned this example of sustainability. I also included a video clip of the production in the application narrative as evidence.

Quick Recap

1. Give context to your proposal idea—tell a story.
2. Ask for action items, not stuff.
3. Learn what's funded so you can find the right program for your idea.
4. Don't give up.
5. Show sustainability—how will you keep the grant activity going?

Reference

U.S. Census Bureau (2016, June). *Public Education Finances: 2014.* Retrieved from https://census.gov/content/dam/Census/library/publications/2016/econ/g14-aspef.pdf

11

Success! Now What?

You got the grant! That's the good news; the bad news is that now you need to implement it. Of course, that's not really bad news, but implementing the grant will certainly be just as critical to your whole project as writing the application was. You don't need advice on carrying out your project idea, though. You obviously have a clear idea of what you want to do with the funding, or you wouldn't have received a grant award in the first place. Instead, this chapter offers suggestions for actions you can take during the grant project period to make submitting the all-important final report easier.

The first and most obvious tip to remember is to actually submit your final report. Many different grant applications remind potential applicants they need to complete final reports from previous years to be eligible to apply again, so apparently, some people don't bother to submit the required final reports. That's not a good idea if you want to ask for money again! Mark the final report deadline on your calendar; it's as important as any grant application deadline, although thankfully, it can be more flexible. I've been able to adjust a report deadline when, for example, I was having difficulty getting bus transportation receipts on time. It's similar to when you need to make adjustments to your original project plan; funders will work with you, but you need to keep them posted to avoid last-minute surprises—for them and you.

I've said earlier in this book that I think the budget is the most difficult part of a grant application; I also think the budget is the most difficult part of successful grant management. My advice is to keep good financial records and document everything. This is important with any project, even if it's not grant funded, but when using someone else's money, it's essential. Keep receipts and note all spending. If you have to adjust your budget, you'll need to explain that in the final report. Also, thoroughly document your project and note the curriculum connections and student participation in your final report. Take photos, collect anecdotes, and use facts and figures to show what was accomplished. The photo in Figure 11.1 is an example of the

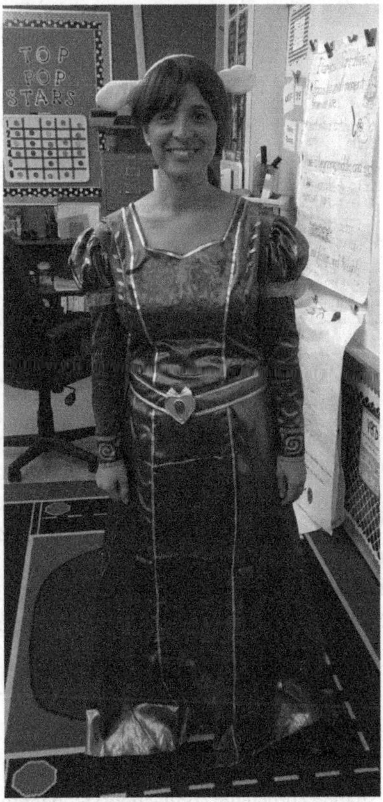

Figure 11.1 Teacher as Fiona on Halloween: Evidence of preparation for a November trip to Shrek The Musical Jr.

kind of evidence to collect. It was part of the final report for a grant from the Southeast Assistance League of Michigan that funded a school-wide field trip to see *Shrek The Musical JR*. This Susick teacher dressed as Fiona, a character from the musical, on Halloween just a week before the field trip. Including this photo in the final report was powerful evidence of the thorough preparation done before the field trip. Even teachers got into the excitement!

Even if you don't include thank you notes from students in your final report, be sure to properly thank your donors after you finish the grant activity. Figure 11.2 shows a typical thank you note from a student to a grant program that funded a 4th grade

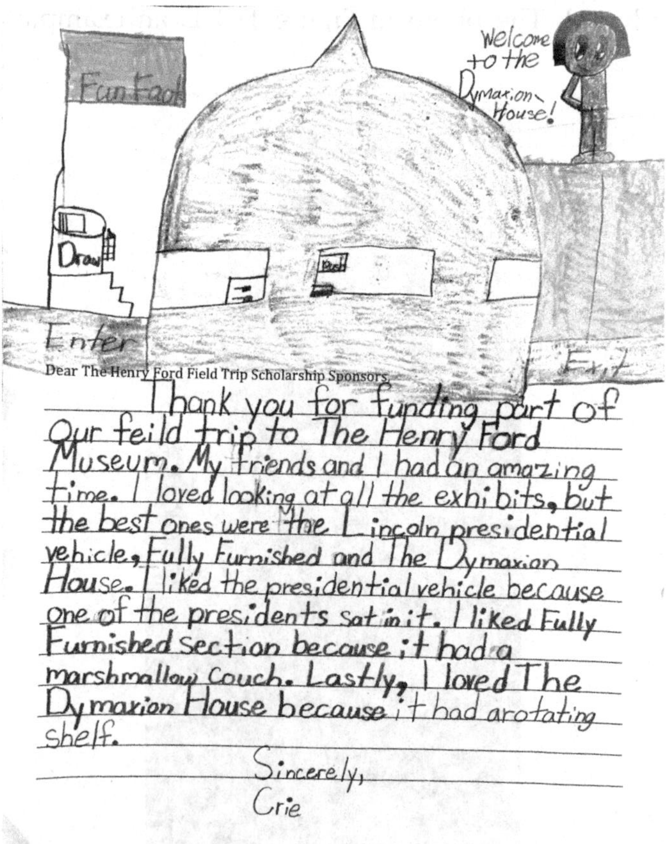

Dear The Henry Ford Field Trip Scholarship Sponsors,

Thank you for funding part of Our feild trip to The Henry Ford Museum. My friends and I had an amazing time. I loved looking at all the exhibits, but the best ones were the Lincoln presidential vehicle, Fully Furnished and The Dymaxion House. I liked the presidential vehicle because one of the presidents sat in it. I liked Fully Furnished section because it had a marshmallow Couch. Lastly, I loved The Dymaxion House because it had arotating shelf.

Sincerely,
Crie

Figure 11.2 Sharing curriculum connections: Student thank you note.

field trip to The Henry Ford in Dearborn, Michigan. Writing such notes is a great way to learn a valuable life skill, and it also gave this student a relevant, authentic opportunity to use some of the academic vocabulary from the field trip. We also used examples of thank you letters like this as evidence of curriculum connections when we successfully applied for the same grant again the next year.

Thanking funders for their support also allows you to continue a relationship with them. That can also be important. After the performance of an original opera funded by an arts in education residency grant with Michigan Opera Theatre, I sent a note to the state legislator who represents our school's attendance area, thanking him for his support of this taxpayer-funded activity. He had visited our school before, so I felt comfortable contacting him. The arts education grant manager in Lansing, Michigan also wrote a thank you note to us after attending the original opera funded by the arts in education residency grant with Michigan Opera Theatre. He doesn't actually review applications, but he chairs the review panels and offers application-writing advice, so I had sent him an invitation to our opera. He was pleased to get it and later told me he only attends about 10% of the final productions from grant-funded residencies because "I can't attend a performance I don't know about." The take-away message here for everyone is to thank funders, give them credit, and get the word out to share your successes.

Giving funders public credit is something I did when I first started implementing grants, mainly because proof of it was necessary for final reports. I'm much more mindful of giving credit now, though, even when it isn't specifically required. Grant awards often come with stipulations about grant publicity; read the guidelines carefully to make sure you do what's required, for example, by sending the funder photos of your project activities or mentioning the funder in any event materials. Applying for grants has made me more aware of the fact that *somebody* is paying for any activity students do—the school parent/teacher organization, the students' parents, a grant award funder, etc. I'm more careful now to acknowledge any and all of these sources of support in school newsletters, field trip permission slips, and event programs, and to even invite funders to come see the good results of their grant awards. For example, Figure 11.3 shows a student with a representative from the Assistance League of Southeast Michigan, a local organization that funded a school-wide trip to see *Shrek The Musical JR*. This student was making a puppet for an original *Shrek* puppet play her class was doing as follow-up to attending the musical. A picture is worth a thousand words, and this photo is powerful evidence of the grant activity's sustainability. Connections were being made to the curriculum six months after the field trip! Even better, we were sharing all this with the grant funders in a final report. Thanking your supporters and giving them credit is simply good manners, but it can also begin and/or continue closer relationships with community members and funders later.

Figure 11.3 Evidence of curriculum connections with a grant funder's representative.

It can also pay off indirectly when you share your successes with others. Getting the word out about activities your students are doing with grant funding can encourage other teachers to give grant writing a try too. In my small school alone, at least five other teachers have received grants to implement their own good ideas. I don't know if my grant writing motivated them, but hearing about their successes certainly inspired me. It helps others to learn that grant money is actually awarded—and it helps even more if it's awarded to people and programs you know.

Success times two: what happens if two different grant applications for the same idea are accepted? What a great problem to have! It occurs because funding is never a sure thing, so people often wisely apply to multiple sources. In one case, when I applied to two different state-funded sources for the same project, I got a rejection notice from the program that offered a lower level of funding. The grants manager at that program later told me our school's application had initially been accepted (so it *was* a good proposal), but it was later rejected when the program administration people learned it had been accepted for funding through another larger, state-funded program. This was a satisfactory solution for everybody since our school still got funding for the project.

What's most important when you get two different grant awards is to inform your funders and check with them before making substantive changes to your initial proposal. You are expected to carry out your program the way it was outlined in the grant application; if that isn't possible, don't hesitate to contact the funders and ask for other ways you can use the funding. That's what I've done when this has happened to me, and it's always worked out. In one case, when we were lucky enough to receive two grant awards for the same project, we were able to take two groups of students on the service-learning field trip instead of just one group. In another case, we were able to apply funding toward additional costs of the service-learning field trip, so the cost to the students was reduced. In still another case, I had to readjust my initial, successful proposal because the whole reason for it had disappeared. After my colleague and I learned that our Learning and Leadership grant application to the NEA Foundation was funded, we discovered the student growth reports on the assessment our English language learners take every spring weren't going to be generated in the coming years. In addition, the workshops we'd planned to attend in Lansing to learn about them weren't going to be offered, either. This is an extreme case, but it shows how things can change, especially because the lead time between a project idea, an application deadline, and the announcement of awards can be six months or more. In this case, it greatly affected our team's proposal; the growth reports we had every reason to believe would be generated and the workshops we had every reason to believe would be offered one year were dropped the next. We solved the problem by contacting the funders to give them reasons why we couldn't continue with our original proposal. We offered an alternative proposal that was accepted. The grants manager told me they really don't want to have to return anybody's grant money; they'd rather work with the grant recipient to find another use for the grant funds that is just as good as the original one. The take-away lesson if you're in this situation is to be as transparent as possible with your grant's generous funders from the beginning. They're just like your principal—they'll support you, but they don't like surprises. Communicate with them early and often if you run into difficulties and need to make changes.

Quick Recap

1. Submit your final report.
2. Document your success.
3. Give funders credit.
4. Keep grant funders informed of any changes you need to make.

12

Review

Now that you have tips for generating good grant ideas and information about writing all that into a grant proposal that gets results, let's try applying what you've learned. In this chapter, you'll judge some actual grant proposal ideas to see if you can pick the winners on your own. You'll also have the opportunity to identify the flaws in a typical "bad" grant application and to analyze what made a "good" grant application successful. In other words, you'll practice looking at grant proposal ideas and reading grant applications the way a grant reviewer would. If you're a repeat applicant to some programs, you will eventually get a chance to serve as either a volunteer or paid grant reviewer. I've done it, and the experience has certainly helped me write better grant proposals, mainly because I got the chance to read so many good—and bad—ones. That's for later, though; for now, try your hand at some simple reviewing:

Let's Critique: What Got Funded?

Here is a list of project ideas submitted to the Kids in Need grant program (www.kinf.org). Kids in Need awards grants of up to

$500 for *projects*, not programs; their guidelines clearly state they like to fund action items. With this in mind, which one of these three actual proposals do you think got funded?

1. A request for $486 to buy ten inexpensive ukuleles and tuners to use with 4th and 5th grade students in my district's newcomer program.
2. A request for $423 to buy materials to construct boomwhackers, plastic tubes of varying lengths that make different notes when hit on the floor. They can also be put into a frame to make a tubular xylophone.
3. A request for $324 to purchase woven fabric loops from a local recycling shop for 3rd grade students to finger weave their own jump ropes.

Answer: Proposal #2 got funded. Proposal #1 was submitted early in my grant-writing days, and it shows. Obviously, I was using this grant program as a way to get stuff—the ukuleles. The curriculum connections were quite weak too. What was I thinking? Both proposal #2 and #3 involved projects in which students were actually making something (action items), but proposal #2 did a better job of linking the project to what the students were studying in science. I pointed out that students would be using math skills when calculating the number of loops needed per foot of jump rope, but what I didn't say (because I didn't want to admit it) was that the students wouldn't be using the finished product to support any other learning. There's nothing wrong with making something to encourage physical activity in and of itself, but given a funder's limited resources, you can see why proposal #2 for the boomwhackers would be considered better. This project actually morphed into one that produced metal xylophones rather than plastic boomwhackers. I had originally wanted to make metal xylophones, mainly because they were cheaper and even more durable than the plastic tubes, but I didn't have a way to cut so much metal pipe. Serendipitously, the husband of the paraprofessional working in my classroom that year had just retired from his job as a machinist in a General Motors plant. After he volunteered to use his machining skill and equipment to help us cut metal pipes for xylophones, I checked with the funders, and they approved the change. This example points out the importance of asking for action items; it also shows a grant proposal can be changed with approval by the funders.

Here are three proposals for the Target Field Trip grant program: (https://corporate.target.com/corporate-responsibility/grants/field-trip-grants).

Target awards $700 field trip grants once a year for spring field trips for students at all grade levels. You've already read the first part of a successful field trip grant application in Chapter 5 and the second part in Chapter 7. With that in mind, which of these Target Field Trip grant proposals do you think got funded?

1. A kindergarten trip to visit Wolcott Mill Farm Center, a demonstration farm and old mill in a local county park system and about 30 minutes away from my school.
2. A 4th grade trip to tour the Michigan History Museum in Lansing, the state capitol of Michigan and about one and a half hours from my school.
3. A 2nd grade trip to PuppetART Theater in Detroit to see a puppet play and attend a puppet-making workshop. It's about 30 minutes from my school.

Answer: Proposal #3 got funded. Proposal #1 for the trip to Wolcott Mill and Farm was probably too ordinary. We eventually did get funding to go to Wolcott Mill, but it was through a different grant program, and we took 5th graders, not the usual young children. Proposal #2 for the trip to the Michigan History Museum in Lansing was also probably too much of the same-old, same-old. Also, this was an expensive field trip because it was a longer distance from school, and the $700 grant would have only partially funded the trip. Target makes no mention one way or the other about wanting to be the sole funder of a field trip as some grant programs do, but it seems to me Target likes to support smaller, less ambitious field trips that don't depend on other sources of funding. I wasn't at all surprised that proposal #3 got funded, mainly because it was so easy to "tell a story" in the application. This trip had a hands-on component with the puppet-making workshop, plus it was to downtown Detroit, where very few of our suburban students had visited. In addition, the students also saw an Arabic-inspired fairy tale, *Mouk's Adventures,* which made the application especially appealing because many of our students had Middle Eastern backgrounds.

MEEMIC (Michigan Educational Employees Mutual Insurance Company) has a foundation that now awards $500 grants to teachers four times a year (www.MEEMIC.com). It also has branches in Wisconsin and Illinois. It's typical of an average mini-grant program designed for individual teachers because it has no special restrictions or guidelines. With this in mind, which of these proposals do you think got funded?

1. A proposal for $1,223 to fund a visit to our school by a mini-version of the local Warren Symphony Orchestra with an instrument-making workshop for all the students afterward. This was submitted when grants were awarded for larger amounts, but less frequently.
2. A proposal for $450 to fund five trips to two nearby senior living facilities by ten different classes.
3. A proposal for $450 to support service work in observance of Dr. Martin Luther King, Jr. Day. The money would pay for two trips to Gleaners Food Bank warehouse so students could do volunteer work there and one trip to nearby Cherrywood Nursing Home to read with the residents and present a musical program honoring Dr. Martin Luther King, Jr.

Answer: Surprise! MEEMIC rejected all these proposals—but other grant programs eventually funded all three. The take-away lesson here is to keep trying. Improve your application, and submit it again and/or somewhere else!

Autopsy of a Dead Grant Application: What Went Wrong?

I have served as a grant reviewer for programs ranging from $500 grant applications submitted by teenage applicants to $2.5 million federal grant applications written by university faculty members. The most important thing I've learned from these reviewing experiences is that no matter how large or small the amount of funding being requested, *grant writers make the same kinds of mistakes*. It's possible for just about anybody to overlook an eligibility requirement, submit a sloppy budget, or write in vague generalities. I've made almost all the mistakes I reference in this book. All I had to do to create this fictional example of a poorly written, poorly conceived Target Field Trip grant application was to draw on my past experience. This "bad" example incorporates many common mistakes grant writers at all levels make, even in short applications like this one. Compare it to the successful Target Field Trip grant application excerpts in Chapter 5 and Chapter 7.

> **Describe the field trip you would like to plan for your students. What's the objective of the trip? Why is it important? Please limit your response to 2,000 characters.**

Do you have childhood memories of going on school trips? Gaining these types of experiences is so important for students. They will gain invaluable life skills too! That's why we want to celebrate the end of an amazing school year by taking our 4th and 5th grade service squad students and safeties on a field trip to C.J. Barrymore's in Sterling Heights, Michigan. These students have been working hard for our school all year. Every year, we take our awesome service squad members and safeties to C.J. Barrymore's to celebrate their success. We want to be able to do this again this year because this project has a lot to offer when it comes to education! This trip will bring an amazing opportunity to our students who don't get to do these types of things! Most of them have never been to an amusement park or been on a roller coaster and may never get the chance to go. A Target Field Trip grant for this once-in-a-lifetime amazing experience for our students will be greatly appreciated!!

Critique

This application starts out requesting field trip funding for a purpose that's not very clear. The writer wants the students to celebrate the end of the year and make memories, but the objectives aren't outlined, and there's no description of what the students will actually do on the field trip. The writer uses jargon without explaining it—the terms "safeties" and "service squad" are perfectly clear to the writer, but might not be terms a grant reviewer would understand. The writer also doesn't do a good job of explaining what C.J. Barrymore's is. We can determine through context by the end of the paragraph that the destination is an amusement park, but this should have been explained clearly at the very beginning of the paragraph. Vague adjectives like "awesome" and "amazing" are overused, as well as the exclamation point! The writer is probably trying to indicate enthusiasm for the project, but it just makes it look like a middle school student wrote the application. That wouldn't be bad if a middle school student had actually written this application, but youth input isn't indicated anywhere. There is also a careless typo, "ever" in the second-to-last sentence of the paragraph, that a computer spell check didn't catch. Finally, the writer references taking students to C.J. Barrymore's every year. Why, then, is the applicant asking for funding this year?

> **How will students benefit directly from the proposed field trip? How will the experience benefit your curriculum? How will you measure student learning as it directly results from the trip? Please limit your response to 2,000 characters.**

Many of our service squad and safeties are English language learners who come from low socio-economic backgrounds. They are excellent students and look forward to coming to school every day. They are hard workers and always willing to try new learning experiences. Unfortunately, they lack the prior knowledge and skills necessary to make connections between what is happening in the classroom and what is happening in the real world outside. If students had access to more educational experiences outside of our classroom, they would truly benefit.

Coming from homes with little or no communication, our students struggle with day-to-day incidental learning experiences.

Thus, they often lack prior background knowledge on many topics. They are visual and tactile learners. Visual information is crucial to their understanding on any subject. Our students need to see and experience the world to fully understand. This field trip will be a trip that the students will remember forever! Research has shown that students learn best by doing. Many of them have never been on a roller coaster, so this field trip to C.J. Barrymore's will give them that opportunity as they learn about energy, speed, acceleration, and much more. They will experience first-hand the laws of motion riding the roller coaster and many other thrill rides. This project will cover the cost of bus transportation for our trip to minimize the cost to families. These service squad members and safeties have done an awesome job all year long! We hope this trip can be an experience to include all of them.

Critique

The response to this second set of application questions is a good example of a long, rambling explanation that doesn't really say anything or directly answer the application questions. The first paragraph does obliquely respond to the question about how students will benefit from the field trip, but it's in the last sentence of the paragraph. A stronger beginning paragraph would lead off with the question stem in the first sentence: for example, "Our students will benefit from this field trip through _____." Plain and simple writing makes it easy for grant reviewers to confirm you've responded to every question and thus give you points on the scoring rubric for doing so. The writer didn't even answer the question about how the results of the field trip would be evaluated, a whole section on the scoring rubric that won't get any points. The applicant doesn't give concrete evidence for many statements—for example, how many is "many" English language learners? How is "low socio-economic background" defined? How do we know the students are "excellent" and "hard workers," and what in the world are the "incidental learning experiences" students are struggling with? Finally, and probably most importantly, the response is describing a half-baked project without any strong connections to the curriculum.

It mentions science concepts likes the laws of motion in passing, but it doesn't describe anything the students will do before the field trip or after the field trip to reinforce these concepts.

Analysis of a Successful Grant Application: What Went Right

Here is an example of a successful grant application for a STEM-related service-learning project funded through a service-learning organization, GenerationON (www.generationon.org). You can see the application wasn't very long—I use nearly as many words describing it for you, the reader, as I did in the actual application.

My colleague's 3rd grade students had been conducting a year-long pen pal project with a 3rd grade class at another elementary school in our district. We were brainstorming a way the two classes could meet for a culminating activity at the end of the year when I received a grant notice from GenerationON for STEM-related service projects. My colleague believed in the value of service learning; in fact, her students had already done some grant-funded service work that year at a local food bank warehouse. Together, we decided to apply for the STEM-related service project grant to get funding for bus transportation to our local nature center to do invasive plant removal. This project idea was such a good one, in fact, that it actually received funding from a second grant program as well, proof positive that a successful grant application needs to not only be well-written, but also carefully crafted. Here are the five parts of the successful application with analysis of what went right:

> **In the box below, please describe your interest in STEM-related service and any relevant work you have done to date in relation to STEM and service.**
>
> Susick Elementary has been establishing a culture of service now for several years. Students are actively engaging in service-learning work—for example, in just this past year, they have

visited the residents of two different senior living facilities 5-6 times, they had a toy drive to benefit homeless children, they had a school-wide food drive, they volunteered at a local food bank warehouse, and they made fleece blankets for patients at a local children's hospital. Last year, our district established a special STEM program for our elementary students. Each week, students have a special 40-minute STEM class that incorporates concepts they are learning in science and math into hands-on projects. The course is very popular with students, but we also want to add a service component to the learning as well.

Analysis

This application nicely incorporated science concepts through learning about invasive plants and service through the volunteer work. It fulfilled the STEM-related grant requirement because students were doing environmental service work and learning about invasive plants. It also didn't hurt that our school had already done a variety of service projects, evidence that grant funders are OK with giving money to experienced applicants, not just newbies.

Applicants must include information about:

What you propose to do, when you plan to complete your project (projects must be completed during March 27-May 12), and the estimated number of youth 5-18 you expect to engage in the planning and execution of the service project. When will you complete your service project? (Must be from March 27-May 12.) How many youth do you propose to engage in your service project?

We would like to give one of our 3rd grade classes a chance to share the service-learning work they have been doing with students in another school in our district. These students have been conducting a pen pal project with another class of 3rd graders at Jefferson Elementary. We want to use the grant funds to invite the class from Jefferson Elementary to join us at the local Troy

Nature Center to pull invasive plants from the park. Together, these 50 students will do service work and also cement the relationship they've built by writing letters to each other. Susick is much more familiar with service work—we want to introduce other students to it too! We have been writing letters to the students at Jefferson Elementary all year. We'll do the service work together at the Troy Nature Center on Friday, April 21.

Describe what makes your project innovative or unique.

Our project is innovative because:

1. It involves students from two different schools who have been building bridges to each other all year with pen pal letters. The service work is a great way for students to meet and do some good for others as well.
2. It helps students show other students how valuable (and fun!) service work can be.
3. Susick students are 42% English language learners and 54% free or reduced-price lunch. They're not the usual students who would think about "giving back," but they are. Not only that, they want to show students at another school how it's done.
4. This project involves actual hands on *work*, not simply fund raising.

Analysis

This project had lots of things going for it, and for once, it was easy to show how it was unique. It had:

1. Sustainability because Susick 3rd graders were sharing their service-learning experience with their pen friends at another school.
2. Connections to the community because the students were performing service work at a local nature center.
3. Connections to the language arts curriculum because it was a culminating activity for a year-long writing project.

It also built on an existing literacy initiative, the pen pal project, and it gave my colleague's students a chance to show their pen pals from another school how much fun service learning could be.

Outcomes/Impact

At the end of your service project, what do you hope to have achieved? Using the categories below, please share with us the intended impacts or outcomes of your service project.

1. We want to introduce one class of 25 third graders at Jefferson Elementary to service work.
2. We want to do two hours of invasive plant removal by 50 third graders at Troy Nature Center.
3. We hope to plant the seed of service work from Susick Elementary at Jefferson Elementary.

Analysis

An additional plus for this project was that the pen friends came from a school where the percentage of economically disadvantaged students was even higher than at our school. This field trip most definitely wouldn't have taken place without help from the grant; we're hoping that it sparks further interest in service learning at both schools as referenced in outcome #3. If it does, you can be sure I'll note that sustainability in future grant applications.

How will you help participating youth learn more about STEM through your project? Which 21st century skills would you like to focus on developing through the project?

Students participating in this project will learn about invasive plant species specific to Michigan. They will learn how to identify these species and how they can be eradicated. Students will also gain a better understanding of the ecological balance of the environment.

Analysis

Everyone on the field trip learned a lot about garlic mustard, the nasty invasive plant the students were trying to eradicate. Figures 12.1 and 12.2 show students doing the service work; these photos were included in the final report. The 21st century skill of collaboration referenced in another part of the application is something we hope to develop in the future. If our partner school does some service learning, too, then we'll know our goal was accomplished. Like all good projects started by good grant applications, this one suggests many possibilities for future projects, thus offering a chance to show sustainability.

Figure 12.1 Photo for the final report: Evidence of a grant-funded service activity. Photo courtesy of Robyn Coppola.

Figure 12.2 Photo for the final report: Evidence of a grant-funded service activity. Photo courtesy of Robyn Coppola.

Common Grant-Writing Peeves

All the irritations listed below didn't keep me from applying; after all, that's how I know about them. Still, I'm telling you, a potential grant seeker, about what bugs me, so when you encounter these annoyances, you won't think it's just you.

I hate grant applications that . . .

1. Ask questions like, "Which adjectives would describe the program or its effects?" at the end of an already extensive

application. I've got an adjective to describe this question—stupid.

2. Require you to set up an online account before you even get to see the application questions. That's a lot of trouble to go through only to find out the grant program isn't right for your idea.
3. Determine a winner through a popular vote online or through social media. That may be OK for some people, but I don't participate in the increasing number of programs that use popular votes. I'm just not comfortable with so much public online visibility, especially for my students. Also, I feel popular proposals may not necessarily be the best proposals. I'd rather apply to grant programs where my proposal will get a thoughtful review by qualified raters.
4. Choose the winners at random but ask applicants to submit written responses. Why do that if the responses aren't even being reviewed? I'd call this a lottery, not a grant program.
5. Ask if you've won an award before. If nothing in the application guidelines prohibits previous winners from applying again, I always wonder why they're asking. Is it just for data collection purposes, or are previous winners at a disadvantage, and they're just not telling you?
6. Require budget contortions. One well-known grant program for teachers requires applicants' budgets to total either $2,000 or $5,000. Nothing is ever that exact, including grant expenses.
7. Don't notify you when your application is rejected. It hasn't happened very often to me (the lack of notification, not the rejections!), but it's annoying just the same. I like closure, even if it's bad news.
8. Require you to submit multiple hard copies of your application through snail mail. The small local grant programs I'm referring to that do this are administered by volunteers, mostly retired teachers, so I understand why they don't have an online submission system like bigger grant

programs use. Still, it's well into the 21st century, and we all at least use email now, don't we?

9. Use online application systems that require you to fill in every blank on the page before advancing to the next page. I sometimes put in random numbers or letters just to fill out the page so I can see the whole application. This, however, can put you at risk of overlooking a nonsense answer since the application system only lets you know if an answer is blank, not if it's nonsense!
10. Use online application systems that glitch just before the application deadline with no technical support available. This annoyance is entirely avoidable, however, by filing at least 24 hours before the application deadline.

Quick Recap

1. Put yourself in the grant reviewer's place when preparing your application. A clearly written grant application will make it easy for a reviewer to see you've responded to every question. This will undoubtedly result in more points on the scoring rubric for your application.
2. Think about being a grant reviewer yourself. The experience will be invaluable.

13

Afterword

Now that you've learned the basic parts of a grant application, read tips for crafting a better proposal, and learned how to write a good final report, you're ready to start writing a winning grant application of your own. Before you do, however, consider these questions and answer them truthfully:

1. Do you have a plan to evaluate the success of the project?
2. Have you carefully read the application guidelines?
3. Do you have experience with the project you're proposing?
4. Do you have partners in this endeavor?
5. Are your students involved?
6. Do you have a story to tell?
7. Is your idea actionable?
8. Is your idea a good fit for the grant program?
9. Are you OK with rejection?
10. Do you have a plan for continuing the project after the grant funds are spent?

When you can answer "yes" to all these questions, you're ready—go for it and write that grant proposal! This book has given you the information and encouragement to do so successfully. Good luck on your journey!

Appendix

Listed below are national grant programs that supported projects referenced in this book. All of them are easily searchable online:

- GenerationOn
- Global Youth Service Day Grant
- Kids in Need Foundation
- Kids to Parks Day School Contest
- National Education Association Learning and Leadership grant
- Roots and Shoots
- Start a Snowball
- State Farm Good Neighbor
- Super Service Challenge
- Target Arts in the Schools (now discontinued)
- Target Field Trip grant

These regional and state grant programs supported projects referenced in this book. They are also easily searchable online:

- Meemic Foundation
- Michigan Council for the Arts and Cultural Affairs
- Michigan Humanities Council